ANECDOTE, HISTORY AND KASHMIR

AND OTHER ESSAYS

Ghulam Mohammad Khan

Made with ♥ on the Notion Press Platform

www.notionpress.com

CONTENTS

INTRODUCTION

In a time when dominant narratives often obscure the truth, it is essential to question, deconstruct, and reimagine the stories we tell about ourselves and the spaces we inhabit. *Anecdote, History and Kashmir: And Other Essays* is a collection that ventures into these contested territories—physical, cultural, and emotional—to uncover layers of meaning, memory, and identity. At its core lies a shared concern for the human condition, seen through the lens of diverse themes such as history, politics, the COVID-19 pandemic, displacement, literature, and the fragile resilience of communities.

Kashmir, the central thread running through these essays, is not merely a geographic entity or a politically contested space. It is a metaphor for complexity—a region whose history is marred by layers of colonial interventions, internal strife, and global power dynamics. Yet, it is also a living, breathing landscape of culture, memory, and resistance. Through these essays, Kashmir emerges not just as a subject but as an enduring presence—a backdrop against which broader human struggles unfold. The collection delves into why Kashmir, with its unique history and collective trauma, deserves a literary tradition of its own, one that captures its complexities and gives voice to its silences.

This work does not confine itself to one theme or region. It traverses the turbulent waters of displacement, which severed not just lands but lives and identities, leaving scars that remain unhealed to this day. It critiques the machinery of modern governance, which disciplines and suppresses, creating societies that are both docile and fractured. It examines the role of language and literature in shaping public consciousness, urging readers to see beyond state propaganda and reductive portrayals. The essays also explore the personal dimensions of displacement, belonging, and the ceaseless quest for meaning in a world often defined by its contradictions.

The essay that lends its title to the collection highlights the role of anecdotes as personal narratives that challenge the limitations of grand historical narratives. Drawing on Gallagher and Greenblatt's theory, it argues that anecdotes, often dismissed as insignificant, offer counter-historical insights by revealing suppressed and humanised dimensions of events. The author recounts an anecdote of a soldier enforcing rigid rules, reflecting the shared helplessness within hierarchical systems.

Across the essays, the collection challenges readers to reconsider their understanding of truth, history, and humanity. It asks uncomfortable questions: how do we remember a painful past without becoming prisoners of it? How do we speak of resilience without romanticizing suffering? And most importantly, how do we envision a future for regions like Kashmir that transcends their current struggles?

At the heart of these essays lies a deep empathy for the human spirit. Whether examining the psychological impact of state surveillance in Kashmir or reflecting on disturbances during the pandemic, the collection foregrounds the lives of ordinary people—those whose stories often go unheard. The essays argue that these voices, though fragmented, form the foundation of any meaningful narrative about history and identity.

The collection also speaks to the transformative power of literature and art. Literature, as the essays argue, is not a passive recorder of events but an active participant in shaping reality. It has the power to disrupt, to challenge, and to illuminate. It can serve as a parallel archive, preserving truths that might otherwise be erased. In Kashmir and beyond, where state and media narratives often suppress dissenting voices, literature becomes a form of resistance—a way to reclaim agency and assert identity.

This collection does not offer easy answers. Instead, it invites readers to grapple with the complexities of our world, urging them to embrace nuance over simplicity, and empathy over indifference. It is both a critique of the present and a vision for the future—a call to engage with the intricate tapestry of human experience, where beauty and despair, love and loss, memory and forgetting coexist.

The author weaves together personal reflection, literary criticism, and socio-political analysis to create a mosaic of thought-provoking ideas. Each essay stands on its own, yet together they form a cohesive narrative, illuminating the interconnectedness of human struggles across time and space.

Ultimately, this collection is an invitation to see the world anew—to listen to the silences, to question the dominant narratives, and to recognise the power of words to transform our understanding of ourselves and the world we share.

– Ghulam Mohammad Khan

1

ANECDOTE, HISTORY AND KASHMIR

An anecdote is a concise, usually personal narrative that communicates a certain point or idea. Anecdotes are normally used to shed light on a person, location, or occasion and can help make difficult concepts easier to comprehend or remember. They often add a humanizing or engaging element to writing and conversation. In their famous book *Practicing New Historicism*, Catherine Gallagher and Stephen Greenblatt assert that anecdotes provide a sense of authenticity and "the touch of the real" that exists both within and outside the mainstream historical succession. The mainstream historians, who usually view individual or small-scale events in relation to a broader historical background, find anecdotes insignificant and "mere rhetorical embellishments" or sometimes "as brief moments of respite from an analytical generalisation". In contrast to the common assumption that considers anecdotes as methodologically inconsequential, Gallagher and Greenblatt propose a theory that regards anecdotes as equally significant as the grand historical narratives. They claim that anecdote could be conceived as a tool with which to rub literary texts against the grain of received notions

"

about their determinants, revealing the fingerprints of the "accidental, suppressed, defeated, uncanny, abjected, or exotic" – in short, the non-surviving – even if only fleetingly. This interest serves the "effect of arousing scepticism about grand historical narratives, or essentialising descriptions of a historical period". They further argue that anecdotes function as parallel narratives that have the potential to puncture the grand narrative sequence of historical explanations and become significant narratives in their own right. Anecdote, therefore, can sometimes be used as a methodological and counter-historical tool to assimilate the multiplicity of voices and discursiveness of memory.

Let me recount an anecdote. I was speeding along the highway, knowing I had just ten minutes left before the biometric attendance system at my workplace would lock me out. After 10 o'clock, the stern officer in charge made no exceptions. Even arriving one minute late meant submitting what he emphatically called "short leave," which sometimes resulted in a deduction from the salary. It was a rigid rule we had grown accustomed to, just as we had grown used to the frustrating halts for army convoys on the road. But that day, desperation gripped me, and I gathered the courage to talk to the army man who had stopped me.

"I'm sorry, but could you please let me through? Our officer doesn't allow us to mark attendance after ten, and if I'm late, my salary will be cut," I blurted. He didn't acknowledge my plea. Whistle in hand, he was focused on directing the vehicles into a line that stretched seemingly for miles, as if the road itself had surrendered to the endless convoy.

Just when I thought my words had been lost in the wind, the soldier, now weary from his whistling, approached my car. He spoke softly, a stark contrast to the authority he wielded with his whistle. "You don't need to apologize," he said. "I never want to stop anyone like this. I understand your situation. But I have to follow orders, just like you. Our officers are strict, and so are the rules. Sometimes I feel awful when I have to stop ambulances, but there's no choice."

He went on to tell me about his own life—his family back home working on sugarcane fields, and his recent marriage, a flicker of personal warmth amidst the mechanical reality of his duty. The convoy, slow and deliberate, began to pass. Meanwhile, I typed out my "short leave" request, ready to submit it as soon as I reached my office.

Before he returned to his post, the soldier, still holding his whistle, said in a quiet, almost apologetic tone, "I'm sorry."

As I continued my journey, I found myself confused, unsure of whom to blame. Was it the soldier, who had politely disallowed me passage despite his own reluctance? Was it me, for leaving home a few minutes too late? Or was it the rigid, faceless authority on both sides that enforced such inflexible rules? Or the convoy itself, groaning defiantly on the road, indifferent to the small struggles of those caught in its path. In that moment, it felt as if we were all trapped in a system of invisible forces, each of us playing our roles, unable to break free. The soldier's apology echoed in my mind long after I had driven away, a reminder that sometimes, in the grand machinery of life, none of us truly have control.

This anecdotal occurrence disrupts the usual flow of history, adding a personal dimension that counters its tendency to generalize and sum up complex events. In considering who writes history and the methods they use, we realize the limitations of historical narratives in capturing individual experiences. This anecdote humanizes a critical aspect of history, bringing in emotions and empathy while challenging simple categorizations of "dominant" and "oppressed." For instance, the soldier who stopped me is part of a dominant power structure, yet he himself is subject to authority and rules beyond his control, revealing the disparities in power even within the dominant ranks. Such narratives puncture historical generalizations by focusing on lived experiences over broad assessments of the collective condition.

Symbolically, such incidents don't aim to counter history but offer alternative perspectives, running parallel to official narratives and preserving the nuances of individual experience. Methodologically, the anecdote leans more toward literary expression than historical; it captures unique, singular moments that history often excludes. Where history concerns itself with the powerful—the structural frameworks of governance, policy implications, and broad societal changes—anecdotes reveal how these structures influence individuals, their relationships, and ultimately, their consciousness.

Literature's strength lies in handling such anecdotes as, for example, demonstrated by George Orwell's essay *Shooting an Elephant*. In this personal narrative, Orwell, a British officer in colonial Burma, describes the internal conflict that compels him to kill an elephant against his better judgment. The essay serves as an anecdotal critique of colonialism, showing how the colonial system oppresses both the colonizer and the colonized. This perspective on colonialism is unique to literature, which captures the emotional, internalized cost of imperial power that history's structural approach may overlook.

The history of Partition in India illustrates this gap between historical records and anecdotal literary depictions. While history provides dates, statistics, and geopolitical causes, literature captures the visceral human costs of Partition, giving voice to individual stories often lost in official accounts. Saadat Hasan Manto's short stories, for example, delve into the chaos, trauma, and moral ambiguity that Partition inflicted on ordinary people. In his story *Toba Tek Singh*, Manto portrays the absurdity of Partition through the eyes of a mental asylum inmate who cannot understand the new lines drawn across his homeland. By focusing on a single character's plight, Manto reveals the emotional and psychological dislocation that numbers and policy discussions fail to capture. Similarly, Khushwant Singh's novel *Train to Pakistan* uses a fictional village to depict how communal harmony was shattered by the violent upheavals of Partition. Through the lives of villagers who are suddenly divided along religious lines, Singh explores the betrayals, guilt, and unexpected kindnesses that emerged amidst the horror. These personal stories humanize the statistics of Partition, making us feel the tragedy on an intimate level.

Closer to home, our regional literature also uses anecdotes to offer powerful counter-narratives to mainstream historiography. Basharat Peer's memoir *Curfewed Night* gives a brief anecdotal account of a 19-year-old militant in Shopian who, inspired by the Bollywood movie *Tere Naam*, grows long hair, frequently follows a girl to her college whom he admires and desires a romantic escape with for a life of peace. Yet the "militant tag" makes this impossible, highlighting the limits and personal sacrifices embedded within such a life. Peer also captures the longing that militants face for ordinary joys, like watching the moon while relaxing in their own homes. Peer writes, "Being a militant wasn't only about getting arms training and fighting; it was also about being excluded from the joys of life. Being a militant was also about the near certainty of arrest, torture, death, and killing." Similarly, *The Collaborator* by Mirza Waheed offers a fictional yet immersive exploration into the life of a young Kashmiri man in a heavily militarized zone. Through his collection of ID cards from fallen militants, Waheed's protagonist serves as a haunting testament to both the personal and collective trauma of living amidst conflict. The "militarized wilderness" metaphor is powerful in underscoring not only the physical violence but also presents a different context to revisit history. On the other hand, writers like Arvind Gigoo, Siddhartha Gigoo, Rahul Pandita, Varad Sharma, and Chandrakanta offer an alternative perspective by documenting the displacement and struggles of Kashmiri Pandits. Through anecdotal depictions that go beyond polarized historical narratives, these writers bring forth the diversity of experiences, reflecting the profound pain of losing one's home and culture, as well as the empathy needed to navigate the layered identities. Both approaches—Waheed's focus on the militarized experience and the empathetic recounting of Pandit displacement—highlight the unique role of literature in capturing complex human dimensions. These narratives challenge monolithic perspectives, revealing how individual stories intersect with broader socio-political narratives, fostering a more comprehensive understanding of the conflict and its deeply human repercussions.

In this way, the anecdote does not contradict history but enriches it, filling gaps and offering perspectives that historical accounts alone cannot convey. By bringing these experiences to light, literature and anecdotal accounts reveal the human realities behind historical structures, creating a fuller, more empathetic understanding of our shared past.

2

THE CRISIS OF THE MOTHER TONGUE: 'KASHMIRI' IN A CHANGING KASHMIR

It is quite common in Kashmir not to teach the mother tongue, Kashmiri, to children. The reasons for this neglect are complex, as the issue transcends language and reflects a broader cultural disownment. Kashmiris often fail to embrace what originates within their own cultural heritage. This includes not just the language but also other cultural symbols. While adopting, mimicking, or adapting to external influences is not inherently harmful, such actions should not come at the expense of abandoning cultural prototypes that define identity.

For instance, recent attempts to revive the *Pheran* (a traditional loose-fitting dress worn during winter) through media campaigns in urban Kashmir have distorted its essence. In the name of modernity, the *Pheran* has been reshaped into something unrecognisable and impractical, losing its authentic Kashmiri identity. Yet, even this flawed revival effort contrasts sharply with the neglect of the Kashmiri language, for which no equivalent movement or advocacy has been observed. The collective disregard for the language cannot simply be attributed to modernism, as true modernism does not necessitate the disavowal of one's linguistic roots. Modernism does not equate a language with backwardness or irrelevance; rather, it thrives on preserving diversity and embracing traditions alongside progress.

The normalisation of this disregard for Kashmiri has become an alarming cultural pattern. Worse still, this neglect is compounded by the deliberate replacement of the mother tongue with other languages, particularly Urdu and English. No language can replicate the depth, diversity, and emotional connection of a mother tongue unless it is itself the mother tongue. The vast majority of Kashmiris do not have Urdu or English as their native language, and it is both unnatural and detrimental to impose these languages as substitutes for Kashmiri. Such a practice not only undermines the richness of the mother tongue but also weakens the foundation of cultural identity and self-expression for future generations.

Since human imagination is vast and boundlessly diverse, language becomes its primary expression. Through language, we articulate the complexities of the world around us, transforming abstract ideas into tangible forms through words. Words serve as the building blocks of this symbolic world, representing an elaborate system of signification. However, the relationship between words and the world they signify is neither predetermined nor fixed. Over time, the usage of a word shapes its distinct identity within a language, an identity that is inherently fluid and multifaceted. Words do not possess singular meanings; their meanings are shaped by cultural contexts and associations, which vary across situations and communities.

The cultural and contextual associations tied to a word or language are central to its usage. This intricate interplay was theorized in the Sapir-Whorf Hypothesis, which posits that language shapes thought and perception, influencing how individuals form culturally specific cognitive patterns. A single word can take on different meanings depending on the situation, the speaker's tone, or even the expression on the face. The signified meaning of a word, therefore, remains elusive and dynamic. This diversity in language cannot be adequately conveyed to children in a language that is not their mother tongue. The richness and subtle nuances of language require an intuitive cultural familiarity that is deeply rooted in one's native linguistic framework.

In Kashmir, where most parents lack a comprehensive understanding of the complex nuances of Urdu or English, it becomes nearly impossible for them to pass these subtleties onto their children. English, which has become a cultural fetish for many, does not come naturally to Kashmiri speakers in the same way it does to a native of London. Similarly, Urdu, despite its regional significance, is not native to Kashmiris in the same way it is to a person from Islamabad. Teaching these languages to children at the expense of their mother tongue poses a grave risk to cultural continuity and linguistic heritage. It is a disservice to future generations, as it deprives them of the emotional depth, cognitive richness, and cultural authenticity that only their mother tongue can provide. Without this foundation, children are left with a fragmented connection to their identity, unable to fully grasp the symbolic and cultural world encoded within their native language.

Language, as Lévi-Strauss argues, possesses a subconscious structure that is deeply embedded within myth, kinship, and cultural values. He famously writes, "Language is a form of human reason, which has its internal logic of which man knows nothing." This internal logic reflects the subtle interplay between linguistic elements and cultural contexts. It shapes how individuals understand and navigate their world, serving as a repository of shared knowledge, values, and experiences.

This unique internal logic exists in its most original and authentic form within a speaker's mother tongue. It encapsulates not just the mechanics of communication but also the cultural essence that binds individuals to their community. A mother tongue carries the weight of ancestral knowledge, local myths, and collective identity, creating a bridge between the individual and their cultural heritage. It is through this intimate connection that language becomes a living entity, evolving in response to cultural shifts while retaining its core structure.

In contrast, second or foreign languages, however proficiently learned, cannot replicate this depth of connection. They remain external tools rather than intrinsic parts of the speaker's cognitive and cultural framework. This underscores the irreplaceable role of the mother tongue in preserving the originality and complexity of language as both a cognitive and cultural phenomenon.

In a mother tongue, we effortlessly acquire a vast repository of words, often without consciously striving to learn them. This natural acquisition is deeply intuitive, as the mother tongue seamlessly integrates with our daily lives and experiences. Along with this vast vocabulary, we also develop unique cultural associations with words, imbuing them with meanings that resonate with our memory, traditions, and shared community values. In contrast, learning a target language is a deliberate and conscious process. Unlike the mother tongue, it does not automatically align with our innate perceptions of the world. Translating thoughts and experiences into a target language often feels constrained, as it lacks the intuitive cultural resonance and depth of the mother tongue. Consequently, the repository of words in a target language remains limited, and the meanings of these words may not carry the same semantic richness they hold for native speakers. This creates a linguistic gap, making it challenging to fully express one's thoughts or engage with the cultural nuances of the target language. Ludwig Wittgenstein aptly encapsulates this experience in *Tractatus Logico-Philosophicus (1922)*, stating, "The limits of my language mean the limits of my world."

The vast repository of words in a language, along with an awareness of their semantic context, is crucial for meaningful communication. Unfortunately, most Kashmiri parents remain largely unaware of the inherent cultural richness and nuanced repository of words in English and Urdu. Despite this lack of understanding, they continue to prioritize these languages, often teaching them to their children as if they were mother tongues. This practice is deeply problematic. The mother tongue is more than just a medium of communication. English and Urdu, while undeniably rich and significant in their own contexts, lack the organic cultural connection that Kashmiri parents can provide to their children. Even after years of formal schooling, many Kashmiris struggle to grasp the connotative and nuanced meanings embedded within these languages. Without an intuitive cultural grounding, understanding the deeper layers of English or Urdu remains an uphill task.

In this scenario, teaching English or Urdu as a substitute for the mother tongue not only undermines the cultural identity of the child but also amounts to a grave disservice. It deprives the child of the ability to connect deeply with the surroundings while simultaneously alienating them from the true richness of the adopted language. In essence, this practice risks creating a linguistic and cultural void, leaving future generations detached from both their roots and the deeper semantic intricacies of the languages they are taught to adopt. Such a loss, given its profound implications, can indeed be seen as a cultural and intellectual sin.

Another critical aspect of this linguistic shift is that when Kashmiri parents communicate with their children in English or Urdu, they often fail to realize that they do not possess complete command of these languages. What they express is frequently a raw, literal translation of their thoughts, which are fundamentally shaped in Kashmiri. This process of translation inevitably results in the loss of tonal, cultural, and emotional nuances that cannot be recovered in the target language. For instance, Kashmiri words like *shoosha* (beloved), *gobra* (dear one), or *gaasha* (light) carry an innate tonal and semantic sweetness that is deeply intertwined with Kashmiri culture and sensibility. Translating these words into English or Urdu fails to capture their emotional depth and the cultural resonance they evoke in a native listener. Similarly, culturally loaded words like *vohow* (vohow is typically shouted as an expression of anger or frustration, often wishing misfortune or ill-will upon someone, especially during heated situations and conflicts with neighbours) are so intrinsic to Kashmiri culture that teaching them in a target language risks misrepresenting their true significance.

Conversely, English words like *serendipity*, *facepalm*, or *saudade*, or German words like *schadenfreude* and *weltschmerz*, are deeply rooted in their respective cultural and linguistic contexts. Their meanings, associations, and emotional impact are nearly impossible to translate fully into Kashmiri or any other language without losing some of their essence. This inherent difficulty in translation is what Umberto Eco famously described as the "art of failure," emphasising that translation can never completely bridge the gap between two languages and cultures because the two are inextricably linked.

The true grace and diversity of a language lie in the mother tongue. Edward Sapir aptly notes that "the 'real world' is to a large extent unconsciously built up on the language habits of the group," highlighting how our perceptions of reality are shaped by the linguistic frameworks of our native tongue. His contemporary, Benjamin Lee Whorf, reinforces this idea, stating, "We dissect nature along lines laid down by our native languages." These observations underscore that a mother tongue is not just a mode of communication but a foundational lens through which we understand and engage with the world. Teaching children in a language other than their mother tongue disrupts this natural alignment.

The Whorfian Hypothesis also underscores the relationship between language and thought, asserting that language shapes our perception and cognition. Losing one's mother tongue, therefore, equates to losing a unique perspective on the world. Vygotsky's Sociocultural Theory (1934) reinforces this, emphasizing that the mother tongue is the first medium through which children develop higher mental functions. It serves as a fundamental tool for communication, thought, and learning. The erosion of this primary linguistic medium could lead to what Antonio Gramsci describes in his theory of Hegemony as the loss of knowledge systems. Gramsci argues that preserving the mother tongue is a vital strategy for resisting cultural domination and maintaining the intellectual autonomy of marginalized communities.

Further, Carl Rogers' Humanistic Theory and Basil Bernstein's Language Code Theory also highlight the irreplaceable role of the mother tongue in human development. Rogers posits that learning in the mother tongue fosters stronger emotional bonds with caregivers and educators, creating a secure and nurturing environment that promotes psychological well-being and personal growth. Bernstein, on the other hand, underscores the importance of the mother tongue's "elaborated code," which allows for nuanced emotional and interpersonal communication within families and communities. This linguistic richness is crucial for fostering empathy, understanding, and social cohesion.

On the other hand, proficiency in the mother tongue significantly enhances the ability to learn and master target languages. A strong foundation in Kashmiri, with its inherent structural logic and extensive verbal repository, equips its speakers to grasp the complexities of other languages more effectively. The unconscious mastery of one's native linguistic system facilitates the cognitive processes necessary for acquiring additional languages, making the learning process smoother and more intuitive. Cummins' Interdependence Hypothesis (1979) supports this idea, highlighting that proficiency in the first language (L1) forms a critical foundation for acquiring a second language (L2). According to this hypothesis, cognitive and linguistic skills developed in the mother tongue are not confined to that language alone; they are transferable across languages. This means that skills like critical thinking, problem-solving, and semantic understanding learned in the mother tongue can directly contribute to better bilingual or multilingual competence.

In essence, a strong command of Kashmiri not only preserves cultural identity but also serves as a cognitive bridge to understanding other linguistic systems. The structural and semantic awareness developed through the mother tongue fosters adaptability and a deeper comprehension of the syntax, grammar, and vocabulary of target languages. Thus, teaching children in their mother tongue does not isolate them linguistically; instead, it prepares them for a broader and more nuanced engagement with the linguistic diversity of the world.

English, in addition to being used as a marker of modernity, has significantly influenced people's sense of identity and modes of expression in the politically and socially unstable region of Kashmir. It has come to symbolise progress and sophistication, while the Kashmiri language, by contrast, has become a symbol of dispossession, inferiority, and cultural stagnation in the collective consciousness. This perception has led to a rapid decline in the use and demand for the Kashmiri language. Tragically, the speakers experience discomfort and even embarrassment when communicating in Kashmiri, further alienating themselves and their children from their linguistic heritage.

Adil A. Kak, a Professor of Linguistics at Kashmir University, provides a poignant analysis of this phenomenon. He writes, "The patronisation and allocation of prestigious domains to these non-native languages consequently led to a decrease in the prestige of Kashmiri, and Kashmiri has played and is still playing second fiddle, if not third fiddle, to whatever held or is holding sway. Presently, in Kashmir, English holds the most prestigious position followed by Urdu, and the last slot is allotted to Kashmiri. This also has, to a great extent, altered the mindset of the average Kashmiri, and his socio-psychological profile also indicates a leaning towards English."

This shift in linguistic preference and the resulting socio-psychological transformation are not merely changes in communication practices but a profound cultural rupture. Over time, this trend risks creating a fragmented community—one where traditional systems of knowledge, cultural cohesion, and a shared worldview are irrevocably lost.

Ultimately, the most alarming aspect of this crisis is not simply that we are forsaking a rich and vibrant mother tongue but that we are replacing it with languages that were never ours to begin with. These non-native languages can never replicate the organic bond between thought, culture, and language that the mother tongue naturally provides. By teaching our children languages that are alien to our heritage, we risk severing them from their roots and denying them the full richness of their cultural inheritance. This disconnection is not just a linguistic loss but a cultural and existential one, with consequences that could echo across generations.

References

Bernstein, Basil. *Class, Codes, and Control: Theoretical Studies towards a Sociology of Language.* Routledge, 1971.

Cummins, Jim. *Bilingualism and Special Education: Issues in Assessment and Pedagogy.* Multilingual Matters, 1984.

Eco, Umberto. *The Name of the Rose.* Harcourt Brace Jovanovich, 1983.

Gramsci, Antonio. *Selections from the Prison Notebooks.* International Publishers, 1971.

Kak, Aadil Ahmad. "Globalisation of English and its Reflection on Kashmiri." *South Asian Review,* Vol. XV, No. I, January 2005.

Levi-Strauss, Claude. *The Structural Study of Myth.* Journal of American Folklore, 1955.

Rogers, Carl. *On Becoming a Person: A Therapist's View of Psychotherapy.* Houghton Mifflin, 1961.

Sapir, Edward. *Language: An Introduction to the Study of Speech.* Harcourt, Brace, 1921.

Vygotsky, Lev. *Mind in Society: The Development of Higher Psychological Processes.* Harvard University Press, 1978.

Whorf, Benjamin Lee. *Language, Thought, and Reality: Selected Writings.* MIT Press, 1956.

Wittgenstein, Ludwig. *Tractatus Logico-Philosophicus.* Routledge, 1922.

3

ROLAND BARTHES ON KASHMIR

Roland Barthes, in full Roland Gérard Barthes, (born November 12, 1915, Cherbourg, France—died March 25, 1980, Paris), French essayist and social and literary critic whose writings on semiotics, the formal study of symbols and signs pioneered by Ferdinand de Saussure, helped establish structuralism and the New Criticism as leading intellectual movements.

Barthes's literary style, which was always stimulating though sometimes eccentric and needlessly obscure, was widely imitated and parodied. Some thought his theories contained brilliant insights, while others regarded them simply as perverse contrivances. But by the late 1970s Barthes's intellectual stature was virtually unchallenged, and his theories had become extremely influential not only in France but throughout Europe and in the United States. Other leading radical French thinkers who influenced or were influenced by him included the psychoanalyst Jacques Lacan, socio-historian Michel Foucault, and philosopher Jacques Derrida.

From the nuanced academic debates in contemporary socio-cultural theories, we have come to understand that society functions as a vast meta-text, where diverse territorial and generic mental frameworks intricately shape the production, consumption, falsification, and reproduction of meanings. This intricate process operates largely at an unconscious level, gradually acquiring an appearance of irrefutable "naturalness." Over centuries, this naturalization of meanings has become inextricably tied to a wide array of, to borrow Barthes' term, "falsely obvious" constructs—myths, images, signs, and symbols that appear self-evident but are deeply ideological. Yet, this overarching symbolic order is not immutable. It possesses an inherently subversive quality, as it has the power to unmask hidden ideologies and expose the subtle ways in which these meanings shape and manipulate collective thought and behaviour.

Roland Barthes, the renowned French literary theorist and semiotician, expresses profound "impatience at the sight of (this) naturalness" embedded in meanings that are meticulously shaped by diverse socio-cultural and cognitive factors. In the context of Kashmir, I attempt to explore how Barthes might have critically engaged with the symbols, cultural constructs, and metonymic representations that play a pivotal role in shaping collective Kashmiri behaviour and territorial consciousness. This essay endeavours to illustrate how Barthes would have deconstructed these symbolic fixities within Kashmiri culture, unravelling the concealed ideological "software" that underpins them. This ideological framework, though often unacknowledged, constitutes the significant driving force behind what in sociology is termed as "social action."

Beauty Plus

The phrase "Beauty Plus," with its potent symbolic representation of society's obsessive fixation on unattainable ideals of beauty, transcends its immediate identification as an image-editing application. Given that our thoughts and behaviours are shaped within a historically complex and structured field of meanings, the need for factual immediacy to challenge such deeply ingrained cultural constructs often feels irrelevant. While the archetypal ideal of beauty may evolve over time, the specific ideal that has dominated our territorial consciousness for generations remains unattainable. Yet, people relentlessly strive for these false ideals. By erasing blemishes and whitening images, Beauty Plus does not make individuals beautiful; rather, it lays bare a dark, repressed world of desire—one in which people aspire to become something they can never truly achieve. Moreover, it highlights the social categorization of colours and their cultural associations, reflecting deeper societal biases. While this may seem like a universal phenomenon, its regional manifestations are particularly striking. In Kashmir, this obsession has reached an extreme, creating a parallel hyper-real space of social relationships where individuals increasingly disown their true identities in favour of fabricated ones.

Hartal (Strike)

The term *hartal*, recently incorporated into the latest edition of the Oxford Advanced Learner's Dictionary, transcends its literal meaning of a strike or shutdown. In the Kashmiri context, it symbolizes a collective territorial submission to an insurmountable boredom, despair, and pervasive sense of nothingness. It represents a complete erasure of the normal, a phenomenon deeply entrenched in the socio-political psyche of the region. Translating the deeply sensitive cultural associations of *hartal* into a foreign language for a different readership risks lexical deculturation, as it fails to capture the lived experience and historical weight attached to the term.

On a *hartal* day, people in Kashmir do not merely choose to suspend their daily activities but are, over time, conditioned by a powerful societal mechanism to spontaneously conform to a collective state of inertia. This phenomenon reveals an internalized pattern of behavioural submission, where individual agency is overshadowed by the inertia of the collective will. *Hartal* functions as a cultural construct that encapsulates temporal gaps of nothingness in Kashmiri existence.

Barthes might view *hartal* as a mythologized sign, one that obscures its historical and ideological roots under the guise of naturalness. It encapsulates the collective consciousness of a region oscillating, much like Schopenhauer's pendulum of life, between two extremes—pain and boredom. In the semiotics of Kashmir, *hartal* serves as both a symptom and a symbol: a symptom of chronic socio-political unrest and a symbol of a society conditioned to find meaning in shared stagnation.

Naukri (Employment)

The archetype of *naukri* (employment) has emerged as a potent cultural symbol that subtly deconstructs the sacred discourses surrounding the institution of marriage, while simultaneously amplifying economic disparity and class consciousness. This archetype reinforces Karl Marx's ever-relevant assertion that socio-economic factors, rather than abstract ideals or moral principles, shape human consciousness. Although often denounced in popular commonsense discourse as a trivial or materialistic concern, the *naukri* archetype wields immense influence in shaping opinions about marriage and the formation of new social relationships.

In its essence, the naukri archetype exposes the deeply internalized social behaviour that prioritizes material superiority over intrinsic human values. It reveals a quiet but persistent denial of human essences, wherein a person's worth is increasingly measured by their economic status rather than their character or individuality. This phenomenon underscores the stark reality of a society that has gradually shifted its focus from interpersonal compatibility to financial stability as the cornerstone of relationships.

In recent years, the conditioning effect of the *naukri* archetype has been profound, altering how individuals and families perceive social mobility, marriage alliances, and even personal aspirations. Barthes would likely interpret this as a mythologized construct that has been naturalized to such an extent that its ideological underpinnings remain hidden. The naukri archetype perpetuates a quiet but pervasive hegemony, reinforcing the material superiority of a select class while normalizing economic disparity as an acceptable determinant of social relationships.

The *naukri* archetype intersects with the constructs of gender and dowry, forming a triad of cultural forces that reinforce existing inequalities in Kashmiri society. Within the socio-economic framework, *naukri* not only dictates marriage prospects but also perpetuates deeply entrenched gender roles and expectations. Traditionally, a man's employment status is viewed as a reflection of his capability to provide financial security, which becomes the primary criterion for his desirability in the marriage market. Conversely, women are often relegated to the status of passive participants whose worth is evaluated through dowry contributions, beauty standards, and familial lineage, rather than their education, ambitions, or individuality. Barthes would likely critique how *naukri* reinforces the binary perception of gender roles, with men expected to fulfil the breadwinner archetype while women are positioned as dependents. This rigid dichotomy marginalizes women's agency and limits their opportunities for self-fulfilment. Employment for women, while increasingly common, is still often seen as supplementary rather than essential. Even when women are employed, societal narratives tend to prioritize their familial roles over their professional achievements, thereby undermining their contributions to the household and the economy. These dynamics reveal how societal constructs are conditioned to appear natural. Barthes would argue that the interplay of *naukri*, gender, and dowry has been mythologized to the extent that its oppressive foundations remain hidden.

VPN (Virtual Private Networks)

In contemporary Kashmiri culture, VPNs have transcended their technical utility to become potent symbols of resistance, embodying the region's enduring struggle against state-imposed internet restrictions. Roland Barthes would likely decode the cultural significance of VPNs not merely as tools of internet circumvention but as metaphors for dissent, subversion, and the assertion of agency in a politically constricted environment.

The adoption of VPNs reflects an ongoing acculturation of protestation, where digital tools take on the symbolic weight of traditional forms of resistance, such as stone-pelting. Both practices challenge state authority, albeit through different mediums—one physical, the other virtual. VPNs thus serve as a technological extension of Kashmiri dissent, enabling individuals to bypass internet blackouts and access information or communicate freely. This symbolic alignment highlights the deep-rooted cultural ethos of defiance against oppression, where every tool, digital or otherwise, becomes a potential instrument of protest.

The widespread use of VPNs among Kashmiris during internet suspensions also reveals a cultural mixture of satisfaction and excitement derived from subverting state control. This satisfaction is not merely about regaining access to restricted information but also about asserting one's autonomy in a heavily surveilled and censored environment. Barthes might argue that this act of subversion, while seemingly minor, carries significant symbolic weight, as it disrupts the state's narrative of complete dominance and control.

The state's response to VPN usage—ranging from physical crackdowns to threats of sedition charges—further reinforces its cultural relevance. By criminalizing VPN use, the state inadvertently validates its symbolic association with dissent, transforming a technical tool into a political act. The harsh punitive measures against VPN users mirror the historical treatment of other forms of resistance, such as stone-pelting, thus creating a methodological and semantic equivalence between the two.

From a Barthesian lens, VPNs can be seen as signs loaded with concealed meanings. While they ostensibly represent a technological workaround, their deeper significance lies in their role as symbols of Kashmiri resilience and the persistent struggle for freedom of expression. The narrative surrounding VPNs is thus layered with myths of resistance, and the indomitable human spirit against systemic oppression.

Sonam Lotus: A Symbol of Science and Tradition in Conflict

Sonam Lotus, fondly nicknamed "Saint Lotus," embodies a fascinating intersection of scientific inquiry and entrenched cultural thought patterns in Kashmir. His reputation as an accurate weatherman, paired with the public's bittersweet reactions to his forecasts, provides a fertile ground for exploring the complex interplay between rationality, tradition, and collective consciousness in Kashmiri society.

Lotus is often perceived as a Tiresias-like figure—both a revered forecaster and a target of skepticism. His scientific forecasts, derived from rigorous methods, are paradoxically treated as clairvoyant interventions, placing him in an awkward space where modern meteorology meets ancient belief systems. This dual role highlights the cultural tension between accepting scientific explanations and adhering to a deeper, almost mythical reliance on divine will as the ultimate arbiter of natural events.

In Kashmiri public discourse, even the smallest inaccuracies in Lotus's forecasts are met with disproportionate criticism. This reaction reveals a latent cultural preference for the infallible and the divine, stemming from an unyielding faith in celestial perfection. Barthes would interpret this as a symbolic rejection of the imperfect yet sincere efforts of science to approximate truth. The collective ire towards Lotus's rare errors reflects a deeper discomfort with human limitations and an implicit bias favouring divine determinism over empirical inquiry.

Interestingly, Lotus's occasional inaccuracies bring a peculiar sense of satisfaction to the public. This reaction can be understood as a subconscious validation of divine omnipotence, where any failure of human prediction reaffirms the supremacy of celestial control. From a Barthesian perspective, this satisfaction acts as a counter-myth, challenging the narrative of scientific progress by reinforcing traditional ideologies that celebrate the unknowable and the uncontrollable.

Sonam Lotus symbolizes more than just meteorological accuracy; he represents the cultural and psychological dynamics that shape Kashmiri society's collective behaviour. His public reception underscores the enduring tension between modernity and tradition, reason and faith, human effort and divine determinism. His figure becomes a metaphor for the larger cultural reluctance to fully embrace science as a means to demystify natural phenomena.

Kashmiri culture is replete with symbols and constructs that shape its collective consciousness and identity. The *kangri*, a fire pot used during winters, represents resilience and adaptability, reflecting both cultural identity and class distinctions. *Wazwan*, the traditional multi-course meal, symbolizes hospitality, social status, and communal pride while highlighting societal attitudes toward celebration and hierarchy. Similarly, *kehwa*, the fragrant traditional tea, signifies warmth and cultural ties to Central Asia, showcasing historical exchanges and traditions. The *pheran*, a traditional cloak, embodies resistance to cultural homogenization and serves as a metaphor for warmth and unity, though it also reveals evolving urban-rural divides. The harsh winter period of *Chilai Kalan* stands as a marker of endurance and traditional wisdom, deeply tied to the rhythms of life and folklore. Kashmiri humour, or *lol*, often self-deprecating and satirical, serves as a coping mechanism against political turmoil, offering resilience and subtle critique of societal structures. The seasonal *Darbar Move*, where the government shifts between Srinagar and Jammu, encapsulates colonial legacies and political symbolism while shaping perceptions of governance and regional identity. The reverence for shrines like Dastgeer Sahib underscores Kashmir's spiritual syncretism, offering a counter-narrative to exclusivity while simultaneously reflecting the commercialization and politicization of sacred spaces in modern times. These cultural constructs, intricate and dynamic, continue to shape Kashmiri thought and behaviour in profound ways.

This exploration into Kashmir's cultural constructs and their symbolic representations highlights the intricate patterns of meaning that underlie everyday lexical usage and social codes. These patterns are not merely linguistic phenomena; they are the threads that weave the fabric of collective consciousness. Through their perpetual interplay, these cultural codes shape not just how individuals interpret the world around them, but also how they define themselves and their relationships with others.

4

UNDERSTANDING RELIGION

When it comes to our region, the understanding of religion is primarily shaped by cultural influences, and the interpretations of religious texts have been deeply influenced by the cultural orientations ingrained within the society. Over time, these interpretations have evolved and transformed, incorporating intricate layers of meaning. Despite these variations, the underlying message of the religion has continued to thrive in various forms. However, every era, often obliquely, has attempted to align religious beliefs with the prevailing pulse of the time, driven by changing technological, economic, and scientific advancements.

In our region, religious debates predominantly arise from cultural, territorial, and psychological factors, rather than a genuine exploration of the historical context in which religious ideas originated or the intended practices envisioned by the originators of those ideas. This cultural and psychological context influences the lens through which religion is understood and practiced, often overshadowing the original intentions behind religious teachings.

Prolixity, prejudice, ego, uninformed debates, and a lack of commitment to reading have infiltrated our culture long back, and these negative traits are now manifested in normalized behavioural practices. It is evident that whenever we engage in discussions about religion, Islam in this context, we bring forth the full force of our reason and intuitive awareness to defend beliefs that are purely matters of faith, devoid of logical reasoning. Paradoxically, when non-Muslims conduct research that unearths truths aligned with some of our beliefs, which were previously unexplored by us, we seize the opportunity to deride these non-believers for not embracing what our religion had predicted or forewarned long ago, neglecting to acknowledge the individuals behind the research.

This collective reaction is an expression of our unconscious predisposition to view acts we ourselves are unable to perform in a negative light. Sadly, we often find ourselves lacking the time or perhaps the inclination to read a book on religion from cover to cover, yet we engage in ceaseless dialogue, forcefully connecting disparate elements to convince others of the unquestionable validity of our perspective. In matters of religion, these debates tend to descend into a murky realm of heightened emotion and ego, where we adamantly refuse to acknowledge counterpoints, presuming that nothing relating to our faith could ever be flawed.

It is truly disheartening to observe that while we approach various aspects of life with careful consideration and prudence, we tend to abandon the principles of commonsense when engaging in religious debates. Instead, we allow our egos to drive these discussions, overshadowing the importance of rational thinking. In doing so, we dismiss alternative perspectives and passionately assert our beliefs without critical examination.

In the midst of religious arguments, we often find ourselves deeply affected when the conversation doesn't align with our beliefs. In these moments, it becomes apparent that our ego is more involved than our rational thinking, resulting in personal hurt. Frequently, when we embark on defending our religion through logical reasoning and discover that the opposing viewpoint appears more cogent, we tend to forcefully assert our own opinion, drowning out opposing arguments by raising our voices to extreme levels. It is important to recognize that the pain we experience is not solely rooted in our love for our religion, but rather in our peculiar psychological state, where we seek to safeguard our own sense of security by fervently advocating for our perspective, regardless of its depth or foundation. It is crucial not to confuse our state of psychological discomfort with our genuine loyalty to our faith.

Moreover, the majority of believers do not rely solely on critical reading of religious books or scriptures to form their highly sanctified perception and knowledge of the prophets or the religious history. Instead, they draw upon a general awareness of oral traditions passed down from generation to generation. This traditional approach often results in the prophets being depicted outside the realm of human context, elevated to the status of angels devoid of desires or human attributes. Such deification amounts to a distortion of the truth.

Similar tendencies can be observed when discussing local seers and Sufi saints. They are often portrayed as otherworldly figures. However, I strongly believe that there is a great need to present them as human beings first and foremost. By showing their humanity, we can better understand and appreciate the difficulties they encountered and the hardships they overcame. In doing so, we can relate to their experiences and strive to emulate their virtues in our own lives. By emphasizing their human side, we can create a more relatable and meaningful connection with these revered figures. We can recognize that they faced trials and tribulations just like us, and yet they found the strength and resilience to overcome them. When we strip away the unreal facade and present them as individuals who faced real-world challenges, we can better understand the true essence of their teachings. We can appreciate the depth of their wisdom and the significance of their actions, knowing that they were achieved by human effort and determination.

Moreover, as practitioners of a religion, it is crucial for us to grasp the fascinating distinction between belief and reason. Beliefs transcend the realm of logic and cannot be confined to the boundaries of reason. When we attempt to justify our beliefs using reason alone, we may find ourselves wandering aimlessly. Belief, akin to the Derridian impossible transcendental signified, possesses inherent meaning that resonates deeply within each individual. It is the essence, the soul that breathes life into our spiritual existence. Although its precise position may elude us, it permeates every fibre of our being. However, relying solely on reason to unravel its true nature would inevitably lead to a fallacious debate.

Our beliefs, irrespective of their origin or transmission, exceed the capacity of reason to fully comprehend. Reason, on the other hand, was never intended to cast doubt upon the validity of our beliefs. Instead, reason and belief harmoniously intertwine, acting as complementary forces that mould our consciousness, much like the intricate workings of linguistic binaries within a system of signification. Both form an integral part of our structured consciousness, working in unison to illuminate the vast realm of ideas and concepts that lie before us.

It is important to recognise that religion is a dynamic and multifaceted phenomenon, subject to the complexities of human interpretation and societal influences. While cultural and psychological factors play a significant role in shaping religious understanding, it is equally crucial to delve into the historical context and the intentions of the original proponents of religious ideas. By studying both the historical and cultural aspects, we can gain a more comprehensive understanding of religion and foster more informed and meaningful religious discussions.

5

WHY KASHMIR NEEDS LITERATURE OF ITS OWN

James Stavridis, the former U.S. Admiral and Commander of NATO in Europe, once made an intriguing case for the significance of Russian literature in understanding not just the soul of Russia, but also its public behaviour, political actions, and even its foreign policy. In his assessment, Stavridis argued that to comprehend the cryptic nature of Russia's governmental policies and its complex political manoeuvres, one must turn to the literary works of Russia's greatest authors rather than relying solely on the analyses of political scholars or diplomats. For Stavridis, the novels of Dostoevsky, such as *Crime and Punishment*, and Tolstoy's epic *War and Peace* offered invaluable insights into the Russian psyche, illuminating the broader political and social fabric of the nation. These authors, he suggested, could provide a more profound understanding of Russia's political actions than even the most seasoned geopolitical analysts. This view vindicates the enduring relevance and authenticity of literature as a tool for grasping the deeper currents that drive political and social action. Literature, often dismissed by some as imaginative or abstract, is, in reality, a powerful

36

lens through which we can better understand the complex interplay between individual lives, collective identities, and political realities. It becomes a repository of cultural truths that are often more revealing, and perhaps more honest, than formal political discourse or historical accounts. The role of literature, as both a mirror and a source for social critique, extends far beyond the realm of the aesthetic, offering access to the lived experience of societies and their historical trajectories in ways that pure politics or history might not. Literature not only reflects a society's values, but also shapes its public consciousness, creating a bridge between individual experience and collective identity. In this sense, it holds the power to inform and even transform political thought.

If literature holds such profound significance, then Kashmir, with its vulnerable political environment, complex history, and challenging living conditions, certainly requires the development of an independent and robust literary tradition—one that would serve as the ultimate reflection of the collective Kashmiri memory. This literature should chronicle the anguish and affliction, the distress and deceit, the death and disappearance, the pain and protest, and the beauty and the beast that have defined the lived experiences of Kashmiris for decades. Despite the region's history of remarkable literary figures and an enduring tradition of literary imagination, there remains a significant gap: we lack a collective body of writers or poets who can comprehensively capture the 'sociological imagination' of the present age in its multifaceted complexity. In other parts of the world, and across the Indian subcontinent, literature thrives as a mirror to social and political realities. Great Indian novelists like Raja

Rao, Mulk Raj Anand, and R.K. Narayan encapsulated the socio-political and cultural landscapes of their times, offering a nuanced reflection of the Indian consciousness. Similarly, Dickens, Thackeray, and the Brontë sisters embodied the soul of Victorian England, while the war poets—Siegfried Sassoon, Rupert Brooke, and Wilfred Owen—wove an invaluable literary fabric chronicling the horrors of the First World War. In the same way, Kashmir requires a body of literature that can act as a chronicler of the region's suffering and survival, one that can narrate the intricacies of our collective trauma, dreams, and disillusionments.

The existing body of literature in *Kashmiri*, however, seems disconnected from the real socio-political fabric of the valley. A significant portion of it leans either towards abstract philosophical musings or is overly romantic, capturing sensual and spiritual delight rather than the lived realities of everyday people. While a few progressive poets and writers have strived to reflect the common man's struggles, the majority remain detached, caught up in esoteric ideas that fail to resonate with the pain and the protest of the people. We have a literary heritage, but why does it fail to hold the same power or resonance as the works of global literary figures who have successfully captured the soul of their respective times? Take the example of Basharat Peer, who, despite his literary contribution in English, feels a sense of discomfort when walking past bookshelves in Delhi. The titles of works about Kashmir, filled with evocative accounts of conflict and human suffering, seem far removed from the rich literary traditions of the valley itself. Why, despite the vast political crises and suffering of its people, has Kashmir failed to produce a literary corpus that can stand alongside the works of other global communities caught in conflict?

This lack of a vibrant literary tradition does not stem from a shortage of topics; Kashmir is teeming with stories—of political strife, human suffering, and cultural disintegration. Yet, the discourse surrounding Kashmir has primarily remained in the realms of history, sociology, and political analysis, rather than being embodied in the form of literature that engages with these issues at an emotional and personal level. We have a vast collection of works on Kashmir's religious, geographical, cultural, and political history, but these should not be mistaken for literature. The distinction between literary and non-literary forms of writing is crucial. For example, while the works of Karl Marx and Jeremy Bentham are important in their own right, they do not belong in the same literary tradition as the novels of Dickens or the poetry of Siegfried Sassoon. The same applies to Kashmir: while we have a wealth of writings on the conflict and its consequences, we lack a substantial literary corpus that captures its emotional and psychological depth.

The magnitude of the Kashmir issue, with its far-reaching consequences on the psychological health of its people, its destruction of long-held social and cultural bonds, and its devastating impact on the collective sense of identity, should have sparked a strong literary response. Unfortunately, the literary works that have emerged, even in the recent decades, have often failed to engage with the deep psychological and emotional truths of the region. Writers in Kashmir have, for the most part, neglected the responsibility of articulating the struggles of the common people through literature. The need for such a literature is pressing and urgent. The contemporary literary attempts, such as Agha Shahid Ali's poetry, have provided some insight into the conflict, but they remain limited in scope and scale. Shahid's works, though powerful, are few, and his exploration of Kashmir's socio-political reality remains confined to a small collection of poems.

Interestingly, much of the new literary representation of the Kashmir conflict comes from writers using English rather than Kashmiri, a further sign of the disconnect between the region's cultural identity and its literary output. This linguistic shift raises questions about the future of Kashmiri literature itself. If we are to truly capture the lived experiences of Kashmiris in their fullest sense, we need a robust, independent literature in the Kashmiri language, one that draws upon the region's rich linguistic heritage and speaks directly to the people. Kashmiri writers need to replace the entrenched philosophical abstractions and romantic imaginings of the past with a sharper focus on the social issues and daily struggles that define the present.

In order to move forward, we must recognize the power of literature to not only preserve the memory of Kashmir's tumultuous history but also to shape its future. Kashmir needs a literature that can immortalize, survive, and glorify the condition of life in the region—one that can speak truth to power and offer hope in the midst of despair. Through literature, Kashmir can reclaim its voice and ensure that its stories, struggles, and triumphs are not lost in the sands of time.

The challenge, therefore, is not just to write about Kashmir's past but to create a living, breathing literature.

In the words of the poet Agha Shahid Ali, "Even the night will be long and the day forever short, but we must, in the end, bear witness to the terror of time." The task of Kashmiri literature is to bear witness—to the trauma, to the beauty, to the resilience, and to the hope that will carry the people of Kashmir forward. Only by doing so can literature truly serve its purpose as a reflection of the soul of a people.

Literature is not merely an "organized violence committed on ordinary speech" or an imaginative search for similitudes in the fantastic universal dissimilitude. It transcends these definitions, serving as a more reliable and nuanced means of representing the complexities and multidimensionality of human life than history or philosophy. It is a perpetual form of insurrection that not only reflects nations but also plays a crucial role in their invention. The American political scientist Raymond Taras rightly observes, "Novels [literature] chart subterranean cultural and political cleavages within society, and have the freedom to do so. Politics, on the other hand, plays out contests in a dualistic and binary universe aimed at overcoming an adversary rather than unearthing absolute truths." This distinction is evident when we critically assess the growing body of literary works produced by writers such as Agha Shahid Ali, Basharat Peer, Siddhartha Gigoo, Mirza Waheed, Sudha Koul, Rahul Pandita, Shahnaz Bashir, and others.

Take, for instance, the example of Basharat Peer's memoir *Curfewed Night*, Mirza Waheed's *The Collaborator*, and Siddhartha Gigoo's *The Garden of Solitude*. These three exemplary literary works from Kashmir delve deeply into the "mini-narratives" that have consistently been marginalized and ignored by the dominant political meta-narratives. The Kashmir conflict, when portrayed through the lens of political history, often overlooks the human lives caught in the crossfire—those who have been forgotten by the larger discourse of war and politics. These works offer an invaluable perspective that the bulk of the region's political histories fail to acknowledge. Basharat Peer's *Curfewed Night* takes the Kashmir conflict out of the realm of abstract political rhetoric between India and Pakistan, bringing it instead into the visceral reality of the lives of Kashmiris. Peer's work is not a fictionalized account of terrorism but a deeply authentic portrayal of the war's realities based on real-life encounters with victims of violence. Peer's own heart bears the weight of the horror he witnesses, as he is overwhelmed by the countless stories of maimed and shattered individuals. This personal, intimate reflection allows Peer to critique the apathetic politics of war and the ideological poison that permeates the rhetoric surrounding Kashmir.

Mirza Waheed's *The Collaborator*, arguably his greatest literary effort, also shines a light on the devastating effects of the Kashmir conflict. Waheed's prose is poetic, descriptive, and finely sculpted, drawing the reader into the haunting lives of those living in the grip of insurgency and counter-insurgency. Rather than focusing on the actions of politicians, bureaucrats, or the often-abstract philosophical musings of Sufism, Waheed's novel centers on the travails, agony, and helplessness of a family caught in the turmoil. The characters in *The Collaborator* are the forgotten ones—those whose stories have been obscured or discarded by politically motivated histories. Waheed's narrative humanizes the individuals whose lives have been deeply affected by the conflict, elevating them from mere footnotes in the political discourse.

Similarly, Siddhartha Gigoo's *The Garden of Solitude* stands out for its "polyphonic" or "heteroglossic" structure, which brings together multiple voices and perspectives to tell the story of the Kashmiri uprising and the chaos it wreaked on ordinary people. Gigoo's novel is notable for its departure from the well-worn historical-political narratives that focus on the exodus of the Kashmiri Pandit community. Instead, Gigoo focuses on the human experience, emphasizing the emotional and psychological toll the insurgency has taken on individuals, transcending the political or communal narratives. By centering the lived human experience, Gigoo crafts a narrative that, while rooted in the turmoil of Kashmir, speaks universally to the experiences of displacement, alienation, and loss.

It is clear that the works of these authors lay down a critical foundation for the literary representation of Kashmir's history and conflict. However, to ensure that these stories are not relegated to the margins of history, it is crucial that we continue to build upon this literary framework. If we do not, the collective memory of Kashmir's struggles and resilience could be lost to future generations, buried under the rubble of conflict and political discourse.

As George Henry Lewes famously asserted, "Literature is at once the cause and the effect of social progress. It deepens our natural sensibilities and strengthens by exercise our intellectual capacities. It stores up the accumulated experience of the race, connecting Past and Present into a conscious unity; and with this store, it feeds successive generations, to be fed in turn by them." This encapsulates the potential power of literature in Kashmir: it can store and transmit the collective experience, connecting the past to the present while shaping the future. By establishing a robust literary tradition that engages with the complex realities of Kashmir, we can ensure that the experiences of its people, the pain, the sorrow, and the hope, continue to resonate for generations to come.

To establish a tradition for such a literature, it is essential to move beyond political binaries and engage with the human dimension of the conflict. Only then can the literature of Kashmir attain its rightful place, not just as a historical record, but as a living, breathing testament to the resilience and humanity of the people who have borne the brunt of its tragedies. Kashmir's literature must evolve to reflect not just the harshness of its political realities but also the rich depth of its human experience—an experience that has too often been lost in the rhetoric of war.

6

TO MY NEWBORN DAUGHTER

Dear sweetheart,

I am writing this letter to you when you are just three months old, when you have just learned to smile – a smile that lights up the world of your mom and dad. I write this letter so that when you find it many years from now, you don't call your parents educated cowards.

When I think about your future, I also think about what you will think about us. Your parents, like everyone else, have grown up in a state of uncertainty. I won't talk about it in detail here because by the time you are able to understand the meaning behind these words, you will yourself be a victim of this uncertainty. I can bottle up several experiences that have seriously hurt me through this uncertainty, but I can't prevent this uncertainty slowly unfolding itself to you.

Our consciousness, my dear, is not entirely our own making; it is an inheritance, a sedimentation of this pervasive uncertainty that defines our lives in this land. You see, consciousness is not an individual choice, much as we might like to think it is. It is shaped by the rules, norms, and invisible boundaries that were already in place when you were born, silently but powerfully dictating how you will think, act, and dream. These rules do not announce themselves boldly; they seep into the fabric of life, moulding us in ways we often fail to notice until it is too late. Over the years, I have observed that each new generation is either coerced or deceived into surrendering to the same old rules, albeit repackaged in new and more palatable forms.

What I am trying to tell you, my love, is that one day, you too will find yourself grappling with this stifling reality. It will press against you, demand your conformity, and test your courage. You may feel trapped, much as I often do. And when that moment comes, perhaps out of frustration or sheer curiosity, you might turn to the small collection of books in my modest reading closet. I can already imagine you flipping through the pages, seeking answers, or perhaps just trying to understand your father. But I fear what you might think of me.

I am afraid that in those moments of exploration, you may take great exception to your father's perceived cowardice. My ambiguity, my silences, my deliberate vagueness in this letter might irritate you. You may even wonder why I couldn't be more direct, more transparent. The truth, my dear, is that I am left with only two choices: to be silent or to be ambiguous. And I wonder sometimes if ambiguity is merely another form of silence—a safer, more nuanced way of saying nothing at all.

When you pore over those books, I fear you may judge me harshly. You may see my choices as evidence of cowardice or escapism, or even solipsism—a self-centred retreat into intellectual pursuits. The eye-catching titles and dense, recondite subject matter may tempt you to dismiss me as someone who avoided confronting the harsh realities of life. But I hope, just as much, that those same books might give you pause. That they might force you to reconsider your perception of your father, to see him not as an antagonist to your own struggles, but as someone who, in his own way, wrestled with the same demons you will one day face.

This letter, ambiguous though it may seem, is my attempt to reach across the years and offer you a piece of my heart. It is not just an explanation but a plea: that you seek to understand, not judge, and that you find the courage to navigate this uncertain world with more clarity and conviction than I have managed to muster.

Books like Antonio Gramsci's *Prison Notebooks*, Karl Marx's *The Communist Manifesto*, Karl Popper's *The Open Society and Its Enemies*, Michel Foucault's *Discipline and Punish*, Roland Barthes' *Mythologies*, Jacques Derrida's *Of Grammatology*, Noam Chomsky's *On Anarchism*, Slavoj Žižek's *The Sublime Object of Ideology*, and many other works of historical fiction or philosophical inquiry might lead you to see your father as nothing more than a cowardly braggart—a collector of lofty ideas he never had the courage to act upon. Or perhaps you might embrace the Japanese term *tsundoku*, imagining me as someone who hoards books, endlessly enamoured by the power of knowledge and love for books but perpetually hesitant to put it into practice.

One day, you may feel compelled to write back to me, questioning my obliviousness to my own condition. "How," you might ask, "could you immerse yourself in these texts— texts that constantly illuminate the existential forces shaping one's reality—and yet remain so paralyzed in the face of those very forces?" I can almost hear the tone of your words, half-curious, half-accusatory, demanding answers from the father you might perceive as both a paradox and a disappointment.

But my sweet little Mahirah—yes, that's the name they finally gave you after much irresolution and indecision—I am writing this letter not to avoid your future questions but to try, however imperfectly, to answer them in advance. Though I fear my response may not satisfy you entirely, I want you to know that this letter is an attempt to offer you something closer to truth than silence ever could.

The reality is, I cannot be as straightforward as you might wish. This is not because I lack the will but because clarity is a luxury I have rarely been afforded in this life of perpetual uncertainty. Still, I believe you won't stumble too much in your interpretation. Language, no matter how ambiguous or elusive, is a mirror of the consciousness that constructs it. And since you, my dearest, will grow up within the same cultural and historical setting that has shaped me, much of what I say—no matter how veiled—will resonate with the shared undertones of our existence.

This letter is my attempt to bridge the inevitable gap between us, a gap that time, experience, and perhaps ideology will create. It is a way of saying that while I may not have the courage to live up to every lesson these books have taught me, I have tried to carry their wisdom in my heart. And perhaps, by leaving this letter for you, I can offer you not just a glimpse into my struggles but a roadmap for navigating your own.

My dear, we live in a blighted land—a place where hope is both fragile and fleeting. When I first learned the art of reading, it was as if someone had handed me a mirror to reflect the many facets of my existence. Slowly but surely, the complexities of my life and the harsh realities of our land began to reveal themselves. The instinct of rebellion spread like a thick fog across my imagination, clouding everything else. The sadistic treatment of our people filled me with a seething, uncontrollable hatred. I felt as though my veins pulsed with anger; a fire fuelled further by the ideas I encountered in the books I read.

The grand ideas contained within those books—those masterpieces of thought and resistance—did not merely challenge me. They transformed me. They planted within me a fearlessness that grew like a vine, wrapping itself around my every waking moment. I thought, if nothing else is within my power, I would at least write. I would write to make sense of the storm brewing inside me, to express the rage and despair that simmered within. These books became a guiding light in the darkness. Their authors, it seemed, had penned their words solely to ignite something within me, to equip me with the courage to write about our blighted land.

It became a passion, an inevitability, almost a contagion. I would wake in the middle of the night, unable to sleep, compelled to scribble down a few feverish lines that clawed at my mind. These ideas, these words—they demanded release. It was as if the best books I read, across cultures and philosophies, all shared a universal truth: good ideas are timeless, transcending borders and traditions. They teach us values that resonate with the human condition in its rawest, purest form.

Yet, my dear, despite the clarity that those ideas provided, the fate of our land grew ever more tangled. Everybody knew why our land was blighted. The causes of our suffering were never a mystery. The solution, too, seemed obvious. But those in power, the warring factions, the vested interests— they never developed a consensus. Instead, they chose to complicate the obviousness, obscuring the truth with layers of misdirection, deception, and division.

As the years passed, this process of suppression became systematic, almost insidious. Foucault taught me a great deal about this—about how power operates, about the normalization of oppression through advanced and seemingly sophisticated mechanisms of governance. What once appeared simple and clear became shrouded in an ever-growing darkness. The suppression wasn't overt but subtle, calculated. The fate of our blighted land, once so apparent, became an enigma wrapped in layers of fear, lies, and manipulation.

And so, those grand ideas, inspired by those timeless books, became a lump in my throat—too heavy to swallow, too painful to ignore. The energy they once infused within me now feels like a weight I cannot lift. The words I once dreamed of writing to give voice to our plight remain stuck, caught between the urgency of expression and the suffocating reality of suppression. My dear Mahirah, I hope one day you will find the courage to say what I could not, to write the truths that remain locked within the silence of this blighted land.

On a cloudy curfew day, when the air was heavy with silence and fear, your grandfather passed away. The loss was devastating, leaving our large family to the mercy of God. That day, the walls of our home seemed to close in tighter, and the weight of responsibility fell squarely on my shoulders. I had no choice but to leave our blighted land, to continue my studies and find a way to support the family. It wasn't an easy decision, but necessity often silences dreams.

As I immersed myself in studies, it did little to quiet the storm within. My heart, pumiced by grief and guilt, longed to bleed ideas—the ones that thundered in the dark void of my imagination, the ones writhing under the weight of the repressive forces that shaped our lives. At that moment, I was presented with two paths: to silently submit to the rules of their world and take care of my grieving family, or to abandon it all and pursue these ideas with reckless abandon, no matter the consequences.

My little darling, I hope you aren't bored by this tale of conflict. I ultimately chose the former path, submitting to the immediate needs of family and survival. Yet, that choice did not extinguish my passion for the latter. It merely pushed it into the background, where it simmered quietly, waiting for its moment. One day, I secured a job, and for the first time in a long while, our disconsolate family was filled with a semblance of joy. The weight on my shoulders eased slightly, but it came with a price.

Expectations and associations, my dear, can make life miserable. No matter how grand your ideas, no matter how fierce your convictions, you cannot simply disown the ties that bind you to others. My family's well-being, the desire to escape the vortex of despair, and the unyielding pull of those ideas—these conflicting forces tore at me with equal strength. They pulled me into a maelstrom of confusion and restlessness. And beneath it all, an overwhelming sense of ennui slowly seeped into our lives, like water into the cracks of a sinking ship.

Life began to feel like Schopenhauer's pendulum, swinging perpetually between pain and boredom. The pain of unfulfilled aspirations on one side, and the monotony of routine and survival on the other. My dear, let me tell you something about jobs. They may bring security, but that security comes with its own set of perils. A job means serving an institution, and every institution functions through a strict set of rules. Over time, those rules seep into you, shaping and consuming your individuality.

And then there's surveillance—an invisible trap that ensnares everyone in the system. It is everywhere and nowhere, subtle yet suffocating. Surveillance doesn't always announce itself with cameras or guards. Sometimes, it's woven into the fabric of the institution, into the culture, the expectations, the unwritten codes of conduct. You think you're free, but every step you take is being measured, weighed, and recorded.

This trap, my little one, is the price of survival in a world where freedom is both a dream and a danger. One day, you may face a similar choice: to conform or to resist. And when that day comes, I hope this letter will help you navigate the labyrinth of your own heart and find your way.

Sometimes, when a piece of sad news would stir the dormant emotions within me, I would step out of my workplace and sit behind a large rock with my colleagues. It was a place of respite, where we could talk about things that weighed on our minds. But one day, to our shock, a camera was installed at the top of the rock. That silent watcher became a new addition to the long list of institutional rules that subtly encroached upon our lives. It was a reminder of the pervasive surveillance under which we lived, a quiet reinforcement of our invisibly tethered existence.

Over time, I developed an odd habit—before speaking to anyone, I would frantically scan the surroundings, searching for the presence of a camera. It became instinctive, a reflection of how deeply ingrained this surveillance had become. Thankfully, they didn't install cameras in the small toilet rooms, though I wouldn't have been surprised if they had.

The rules, my dear, were not just policies written on paper. They shaped us, moulded us, and controlled us in ways that were both subtle and overwhelming. The impact on individual behaviour was inescapable. Despite this, I made a conscious choice to align myself with those who toiled tirelessly, those who dreamed of carving out a slice of peace amid the chaos. It wasn't because I lacked courage or conviction but because, like everyone else, I longed for a semblance of normalcy outside the cacophony of noise and confusion.

The streets, Mahirah, were their own kind of paradox. On one day, they buzzed with the hum of commerce and activity, and on another, they reverberated with chants, slogans, and the clash of stones against shields. This volatile rhythm had become so familiar that people adjusted their lives to its unpredictable cadence. It was a strange adaptation, a kind of resilience born from necessity rather than choice.

With the money I earned, I helped my family build a new house—a small sanctuary amid this turmoil. For the first time, I had a room of my own to sleep in, a luxury that felt both surreal and deeply gratifying. Even more fulfilling was seeing the smile return to the tired, sunken cheeks of my aging mother. It was a fleeting victory against the overwhelming tide of despair.

What can you do to such associations, my dear? They are ties that bind, often as much a source of joy as of anguish. Sensitive souls like mine are particularly vulnerable to the weight of these connections. They tug at your heart, reminding you of your responsibilities, your limitations, and the constant tension between duty and desire. This state of undecidability—of being caught between what you owe to others and what you owe to yourself—is a torment unlike any other. It is a persistent echo of what you are versus what you could have been, a relentless cycle of self-recrimination.

And so, life continued in this suspended state. The people, forced into an ignoble surrender to circumstances, were left bewildered and lost. Confusion became their companion, as the line between resilience and resignation blurred. My dear, it is this maze of contradictions that I write to you about—not to dishearten you but to prepare you for the labyrinth of life in our blighted land.

Meanwhile, I travelled to many places across our blighted land. Each journey was an attempt to understand its pulse, to connect with its people and their stories. I met countless individuals and had many heart-warming conversations. Yet, I noticed a curious and recurring pattern—almost every conversation, no matter how vibrant or meaningful, would inevitably end with the same familiar phrase: "Wen kya karo?" ("What to do now?"). It wasn't deliberate; people seemed utterly unaware that this little phrase encapsulated their collective despair and an underlying sense of helplessness. It was a silent testimony to the shared uncertainty that hung over their lives like an unrelenting shadow.

Then came the COVID-19 pandemic, which deepened this silence, pressing it further into every corner of our lives. The already fragile rhythm of life grew heavier, slower. During this time, though, something beautiful happened—I married your mom on a bright October day. There's much I'm skipping here because, honestly, not much has changed. In our blighted land, every day is often just another shadow of the one before.

But amidst the monotony, my dearest, life blessed me with you. You became the light in our otherwise dim existence. I've come to realize that the true beauty of life is often hidden in its smallest moments. It takes time for these tiny fragments to coalesce into something larger, something meaningful. They may not complete us, but they do give us fleeting moments of happiness, moments when the pendulum of life swings not just between pain and boredom but between hope and joy.

Every evening, when I return from work, your mom places you in my lap. You gaze at me for a moment, studying my face, and then suddenly, your face breaks into a radiant smile. That smile, my little Mahirah, is like a key that temporarily unlocks the chains of my external world. In that moment, all my burdens, anxieties, and associations dissolve. Life doesn't seem so heavy; it feels bearable, even beautiful.

But then, after dinner, when you're fast asleep, your mom often reads me a sad piece of news from her phone, and the night turns into a torment. The darkness of pain returns, pulling me back into the same void I had momentarily escaped. And yet, it is these associations—your smile, your mom's unwavering presence—that tether me to life. They are the lifelines that keep pulling me back, reminding me of the fragile beauty that persists even in despair.

Life here, my dear, is suspended in a perpetual state of uncertainty, caught between these extremes. I often wonder where I truly belong, whether the choices I've made are right or wrong. It's a question that gnaws at me; one I have no clear answer to.

This letter, Mahirah, is my attempt to explain myself to you. Someday, when you're older, you'll read these words and decide for yourself. Perhaps you'll understand, perhaps you won't. Either way, I hope this letter gives you a glimpse of my heart, my struggles, and my love for you.

With all my love,

Your Dad

7

THE POLITICS OF LANGUAGE IN KASHMIR

In contemporary literary theory, nothing seems to halt the ever-evolving thematic of fluidity, arbitrariness, or the slipperiness of the signified in human languages. Language, with its enigmatic complexities and innate propensity to generate a series of ambiguous and often conflicting meanings, has always been an interesting source of intrigue and inquiry. Its profound influence on human behaviour, intertwining with the nervous, endocrine, and psychological frameworks, has resulted in a ceaseless proliferation of theoretical paradigms attempting to decode its mysteries. Historically, language's inherent duality, deceptiveness, and paradoxical nature have made it a powerful tool for those in authority, wielded as a weapon of public oppression, societal division, and systemic subordination.

Language is, by nature, power-friendly; it aligns itself with dominance, amplifying the voice of the powerful while silencing or distorting that of the oppressed. For the powerful, language becomes a megaphone, spilling over with layered meanings, resonating across time and memory, its audibility etched into the collective consciousness. For the marginalized, however, it loses its semantic richness and metaphorical elegance, devouring its own anatomy of meaning and reducing their narratives to mere echoes. In our shifting global political landscape, the deliberate manipulation of language's intrinsic complexities has deepened. It now shapes not only overt communication but also the subtle assumptions, biases, and codifications that underpin political systems, influencing individual and collective behaviours in profound and often unnoticed ways.

From Abraham Lincoln to Donald Trump, the semantic and formal structure of the political lexicon has undergone significant transformation, mirroring the evolution of interpretative communities within a changing electorate. Lincoln's rhetoric, rooted in appeals to unity, moral clarity, and the ideals of democracy, contrasts sharply with Trump's populist and polarizing language. Trump's scorched-earth political lexicon—characterized by terms like "radical Islamic terrorism," "crooked Hillary," "drain the swamp," and "lying Ted"—not only exemplifies a shift in political communication but also highlights the adaptability of language to the socio-political climate of its time.

In Lincoln's America, such combative and reductionist terminology would likely have been met with scepticism or disdain, as the electorate of that era sought rhetorical appeals grounded in reason and statesmanship. Conversely, Trump's rhetoric thrives in the contemporary media-saturated, ideologically fractured environment, resonating deeply with segments of the American collective sensibility. By framing himself as a saviour against perceived threats—whether international terrorism, unchecked immigration, or corporate exploitation—Trump taps into the fears, frustrations, and aspirations of a populace seeking straightforward answers to complex problems. This transformation in the political lexicon reflects not just a change in leadership styles but also a broader evolution in how political discourse engages with the emotional and psychological dimensions of an electorate shaped by rapid globalization and information overload.

In India, the BJP government's conspicuous upsurge in political vocabulary serves as a carefully orchestrated attempt to critique the so-called "political paralysis" of previous regimes, rekindle a sense of India-first nationalism, and gently persuade people to embrace the promise of "achhe din aane waale hai." Aware of the nation's cultural heterogeneity and the diverse political conditions across its states, politicians craft their linguistic strategies with precision, tailoring their rhetoric to regional contexts and electoral needs. The vocabulary of Adityanath, while contrived, is strategically timed and contextualized for Uttar Pradesh, just as Owaisi's blunt and provocative lexicon is calculated to resonate in Hyderabad.

Ahead of elections, the lexicons of political figures undergo striking transformations. Omar Abdullah, for instance, modifies his rhetoric to capitalize on Kashmir's political turmoil, cleverly branding Modi-Shah politics with the acronym "ODOMOS" (Overdose of Only Modi Only Shah), aiming to entangle the electorate in linguistic play while steering attention away from substantive issues. Meanwhile, figures like Anant Hegde, Sakshi Maharaj, Subramanian Swamy, and Farooq Abdullah craft their rhetoric into potent tools, deploying ominous metaphors and polarizing language centred on Ram Mandir, cows, or Pakistan to stoke emotional and ideological fervour.

During elections, this linguistic manipulation often descends into its basest form. Pakistan is painted as a menacing political "other," an existential threat to the nation's "integrity." Kashmir becomes a rhetorical battlefield, depicted as a site where soldiers shed blood for an inflated sense of patriotism, while Ram Mandir is invoked as a civilizational impasse, perpetuating deep-seated divisions. This lexical histrionics, aimed at arousing the electorate's sentiments, reduces complex national issues into simplistic and polarizing narratives, prioritizing electoral gains over meaningful political discourse.

In Jammu and Kashmir, the political lexicon is uniquely convoluted, reflecting the deeply entrenched regional narrative divergence surrounding the conflict. This complexity stems from a spectrum of rhetoric: some leaders exploit blood and faith to mobilize people, relying on primal emotions rather than reasoned discourse. Such rhetoric requires no elaborate persuasion, yet paradoxically incites a collective willingness to endure pain and futility, perpetuating cycles of despair. Others, however, have mastered the art of hollow promises, speaking words that bear no connection to their actual intentions or actions. Their brazen audacity lies in their ability to assure the public of reversing political calamities they themselves have instigated, without an iota of accountability or shame.

The former Chief Minister exemplifies this duplicity, rallying a contrived and putrid lexicon around an ideal of peace she had a hand in eroding. Rather than self-reflection or atonement, her rhetoric reeks of political opportunism and a shameless disregard for the collective suffering of the people. Such conduct not only erodes trust but also deepens the alienation felt by the populace.

More troubling is the extent to which the people's suffering and the true nature of the region's political crisis have been obfuscated and diluted by the deceptive employment of political language. Over decades, politicians have used this lexicon to manipulate perceptions, erode identities, and drown the pressing realities of the conflict in a sea of calculated ambiguity. In doing so, they have perpetuated a cycle of non-existence and non-identity for the people, reducing their plight to a tool for political manoeuvring.

Shah Faesal's resignation from the Indian Administrative Service (IAS) and subsequent foray into politics created significant ripples in Jammu and Kashmir's socio-political sphere. His adept manipulation of language—intentional and carefully executed—helped him dominate media narratives and position himself as a transformative figure. Through calculated rhetoric in televised debates and interviews, he managed to pre-emptively counter criticisms, projecting an image of moral and political awakening. This linguistic strategy allowed him to retain a veneer of credibility, despite the inherent contradictions in his decision.

In his bureaucratic role, Faesal arguably had a more tangible platform to serve the people, particularly the underprivileged, with honesty and efficacy. Politics in Jammu and Kashmir, however, is deeply entrenched in servility and opportunism, offering little scope for genuine transformation aligned with the aspirations of the suffering majority. This has been witnessed before in figures like Muzaffar Beig and Haseeb Drabu, whose initial intellectual promise waned as they became embroiled in the compromises of state politics.

The political landscape in Jammu and Kashmir, shaped heavily by a disciplinarian, Delhi-centric policy framework, often renders personal integrity irrelevant. Words may offer the illusion of agency, but they rarely translate into substantive action within this system. The public has observed this recurring pattern: lofty promises give way to shifting allegiances, while the manipulation of political rhetoric remains constant. Ultimately, such dynamics deepen disillusionment among the populace, further eroding trust in political figures and institutions.

In a region fraught with perpetual turmoil, the lexicon of the powerful often cloaks repressive measures in a guise of normalcy. Terms like "precautionary measure" carry an insidious weight, signifying an outright clampdown on civil liberties—curfews, the closure of schools and colleges, internet shutdowns, and the cascading suffering that follows. This euphemistic vocabulary, while seemingly benign, effectively silences dissent and paralyzes everyday life under the pretext of maintaining order.

On the other hand, the lexicon of dissent—manifested in calls for protests like *chalo*—is no less potent in its ramifications. These words, often symbolic of resistance, carry a dangerous undertone, igniting unrest that can lead to loss of life and perpetuating the cycle of violence. Both lexicons, though ideologically opposed, seem to converge in their capacity to disrupt lives and quench no one's thirst for peace or justice.

As elections loom, this rhetorical warfare is poised to intensify, with linguistic euphemisms likely taking a more insidious turn. The spectre of another "collective epileptic blackout," a metaphor for the paralysis of democracy and reason during election cycles, looms large. Such outcomes, tragically predictable, are emblematic of a political culture that thrives on manipulation, fostering despair rather than hope for meaningful change.

8

A DISCOURSE ON LITERATURE, POLITICS AND KASHMIR

In the region of Kashmir, a historical-cum-political event in 2019 has altered the collective perception of the purpose, means, and future of resistance. The manner in which it unfolded was unexpected and abrupt. Its impact has been both undesirable and overbearing. It abruptly severed the region's connection to its past. The collective memory was ransacked. The region entered an era of oppressive silence; a time with an excessive emphasis on clear-cut instructions and directives, spitefully disciplinary. It didn't bring less grief, but rather more silence. It bore a resemblance to a nighttime snowfall. It ravaged everything with silence. As I reflect on the changes under this new peculiar system, I am reminded of a recent conversation I had with a Professor who taught me when I had just begun to study Sociology.

"Hello, this is Professor Aflak Padder," the Professor said in a stern tone over the phone. "Am I talking to Mr. Junejo? " I responded without hesitation, "Yes." During our classes, Professor Aflak would frequently refer to me as "Junejo." Regrettably, my peers would exploit it with a sickening enthusiasm, mockingly. I still haven't looked into the real meaning behind the term "Junejo." Certain terms have a greater significance when their precise meaning is unknown. "Rumours are circulating about your excessive chatter regarding trivial matters," he asserted. "Come to my place tomorrow. It is a matter of great importance that necessitates further discussion." He abruptly disconnected the call, which left me feeling uncertain and impelled to rummage through my memories.

I will refrain from delving into the specifics of how a pack of ravenous dogs brutally tore the hem of my *pheran* in the narrow, elongated lane that led to the Professor's residence on that misty morning.

He murmured, flicking off the cigarette ash from his *pheran*, "Still young, Junejo." His physical appearance looked lacklustre and frail, except for his engaging conversational energy and lively, beaming eyes. An overgrown salt and pepper moustache nearly concealed his upper lip. "I recently encountered an article of yours that was published in a local magazine that is a dime a dozen." In his opinion, it was merely a piece of garbage, as it was overly simplistic. "Such writing is no longer sufficient for our survival. It should adopt a Barthesian perspective, operating in a circuitous and oblique domain where meanings are ambiguous and paradoxical, yet not overtly direct", he continued, his brow furrowing with more pronounced lines of concern. "Otherwise, we might as well abandon the craft of writing."

I hurriedly concealed the tattered remains of my *pheran*, responding, "I will be more cautious in the future, sir." My legs continued to tremble with uneasiness. In the interim, the Professor let out a belch and sluggishly shifted to his left, resting his back against a mound of bedding in the corner. "Your writing style appears somewhat unremarkable." Literature, in his opinion, instructs us to defamiliarize the ordinary in a variety of ways, thereby transforming it into something extraordinary, intriguing, and indirect. "You may become a victim of surveillance, which is a matter of concern for me. Perhaps, I wouldn't have had to face the unrelenting condemnation that I did in my old age, had I mastered the art of veiling or camouflaging my pain, or the pain of anyone, behind the mask of a metaphor or skillfully employed the detached authorial stance in which the author is dissolved. I was also summoned recently and subjected to physical abuse for my candour in my writing. An additional concern is the obsolete monological interpretation or appreciation of literature. Rather than recognising the inherent diversity of voices within the text, our interpretations often concentrate on locating and categorising the author," the Professor explained, wheezing out loud. He made an awkward attempt to grab the spittoon placed to his right.

"I am sorry to hear that. I understand that these are difficult times, but it is genuinely disheartening to see a professor receiving abuse for simply exercising the inherent nature of his profession. Nevertheless, I am compelled to inquire: is it genuinely feasible for a metaphor or linguistic ambiguity to circumvent what you refer to as the "trap of surveillance"? The Professor removed ashes from the glowing embers in his *kanger* as thick curls of smoke escaped his lips. "You see," he began, "you must imbue language with a level of complexity that impedes the reader from easily classifying the writer. You must be aware of the hazardous categories to which I am alluding. It is permissible if they characterise you as impalpable, recondite, or enigmatic."

"I am of the opinion that our readers are neither naive nor uninformed. For example, Orwell's *Animal Farm*, a beast fable, did not diminish his status as a democratic socialist." I responded, "Writing within the realm of fiction should, in theory, offer sufficient protection against the dangers of surveillance for a writer."

"Well, fiction does not provide immunity to the act of writing anything and expecting it to go unnoticed." He opined that surveillance does not differentiate between genres; it merely targets specific messages. Additionally, fiction is not merely a casual representation of human imagination or a whimsical indulgence. It has the capacity to explore social truths in a more profound manner than newspaper editorials. Dickens, Thackeray, and the Bronte sisters have conveyed to the world more political and social truths than all the professional politicians, publicists, and moralists combined. Even the great Karl Marx acknowledged that.

"Sir, I am merely a regular student and an occasional writer. What is the purpose of engaging in discussions about the use of writing techniques that create ambiguity in meaning? It can be a safer option to discontinue writing wholly. I am referring to the fact that I will no longer be writing. I had consistently maintained the conviction that writing was a harmless and safe pursuit. It is truly disheartening to know that writing can inflict such ignominious torment upon a respected and elderly professor like yourself."

"No, no, no," the elderly Professor grumbled, his voice brimming with annoyance. "You are a spineless, incompetent person! I am telling you that they once subjected me to a severe beating. For weeks, my swollen behind caused such discomfort! I would have advised you over the phone to refrain from writing again if this ordeal had crushed me to complete surrender. It is quite straightforward, isn't it? I do not wish for you to relinquish something today, solely because I am concerned. I don't want you to harbour feelings of resentment towards me tomorrow. My dear, writing is indispensable. I do not wish for you to abandon it. I may be unable to give precise advice; however, I urge you to experiment with your writing methods. It is possible that magical realism could be effective. Essentially, our writing is an anecdotal record of history that disrupts the established and normalised narrative sequence of our past. The approach that Gallagher and Greenblatt advocated in *Practicing New Historicism*. Therefore, the process of writing for us will always be characterised by ambiguity." The Professor smoked relentlessly, leaving a shroud-like thin cover of smoke in the recesses of the spacious hall.

"We become our own adversaries when it comes to writing, as we find it difficult to write about ourselves. Diverting to unrelated themes would insult the fundamental nature of writing. We are left with two choices: either to discontinue writing wholly or, as you suggest, to adopt new writing methods and learn from them."

"Dear Junejo, our subject is undoubtedly difficult; however, the absence of writing would gradually erode the very essence we seek to explore. You..." The room was abruptly silent with an unexpected knock at the door.

The conversation reflects a growing sense of insecurity surrounding the act of writing directly about politics in Kashmir. This insecurity has contributed to a noticeable decline in the production of serious literary work, as writers increasingly feel constrained in addressing the complex political realities of the region. In the short section discussing the growing literary culture in the English language in his book *Kashmir: Rage and Reason*, Kashmiri journalist Gowher Geelani admits that despite having a thriving community of writers, Kashmir still lacks a robust literary portrayal of the conflict. He calls it a 'narrative vacuum'.

Literature naturally evolves using the articulation of human experiences, emotions, and adversities. Institutional repression, regardless of its invisibility or subtlety, cannot entirely suppress this urge. Historically, literature has endured through oral traditions, encoded language, and clandestine activities. The enduring existence of literary forms, despite restriction, demonstrates the unyielding human desire for expression. In totalitarian regimes such as Soviet Russia or Mussolini's Italy, literature persisted through samizdat, exile, and allegory. The act of writing constitutes a form of resistance against the state's repressive forces.

Literature is inextricably linked to the political framework that influences human existence. Each historical period, governmental system, or social movement influences literature, either through direct involvement or indirect representation. By engaging with the political, literature does not only "supplement" the prevailing narrative but offers an essential critique. It encapsulates subtleties, paradoxes, and perspectives sometimes overlooked or marginalised in official narratives. Works like George Orwell's *1984* and Salman Rushdie's *Midnight's Children* function as alternative histories, contesting official narratives and revealing political motives.

The effectiveness of literature is in its capacity to reflect, critique, and shape governmental policies and actions. It presents a lens to examine the apathy or distortions of state authority, offering a platform for the unification of public consciousness. Writers such as Vaclav Havel in Czechoslovakia and Nadine Gordimer in apartheid South Africa wrote their works in opposition to oppressive regimes. They introduced into public debate the unarticulated desires, anxieties, and aspirations of the masses, compelling the state to reckon with the true values of its citizens.

Writers and artists have historically resisted persecution, surveillance, and state intrusion. Writing under observation constitutes a method of survival and resistance. Literary traditions, particularly during periods of oppression, are frequently upheld by those who choose not to keep silent, as demonstrated by the works of Aleksandr Solzhenitsyn and Pablo Neruda. This long tradition of resistance enhances both the survival and progress of literature, imbuing it with complexities caused by the conflict. To relinquish would entail limiting this essential strand of human resilience and creative perseverance.

In spite of technical progress or governmental efforts to curtail free expression, the written word persists.

Literature is among the rare creative forms that can be transmitted over generations, even in the most oppressive regimes. It safeguards the collective memory, unexpressed dissatisfaction and aspirations of individuals, enduring long after the regimes that attempted to suppress them have collapsed. Writers who persevere contribute to this lasting legacy, guaranteeing that future generations know both the anguish of oppression and the strength of defiance. There are numerous literary pieces that serve as alternative or parallel narratives. Aleksandr Solzhenitsyn's *The Gulag Archipelago* exposes the atrocities perpetrated in Soviet labour camps during Stalin's rule. Notwithstanding the state's efforts to stifle dissent and manipulate narratives, Solzhenitsyn employed his literature to chronicle the anguish of millions. His work was prohibited in the USSR, although it was disseminated clandestinely (samizdat) and ultimately became a significant instrument that aided in the collapse of the Soviet state. This illustrates how literature may endure despite suppression and how it can expose the bias and brutality of prevailing state narratives. Gabriel Garcia Márquez's *One Hundred Years of Solitude*, predominantly regarded as a work of magical realism, has political subtexts that mirror Colombia's tumultuous history and the repercussions of colonialism and imperialism in Latin America. Márquez's work quietly exposes the political system and the cyclical character of history, illustrating how literature can intertwine political and historical realities into narratives that transcend their immediate setting. The novel functions as a counter-narrative to prevailing histories, revealing the violence and exploitation frequently omitted from official records. Chinua

Achebe's *Things Fall Apart* challenges the colonial tropes that pervaded African literature. Achebe narrates the story from the viewpoint of the Igbo people, offering an alternative perspective to the European depiction of African cultures as "primitive" and "barbaric." His work demonstrates how literature may contest the prevailing narrative (namely, colonialism) and affirm the agency of marginalised voices. Achebe emphasises the political dimension of storytelling and its function in transforming public awareness of African identity and history. Jean-Paul Sartre's *What Is Literature?* examines the imperative for literature to connect with political realities. He contends that writers are "condemned to freedom" and cannot evade the obligation of confronting the social and political settings that shape human experience. Sartre's work emphasises that literature is inextricably linked to the political realm and must engage with it, since it influences public opinion and understanding of history. Similarly, George Orwell's *Animal Farm* and *1984* exemplify writing that opposes centralised power. *Animal Farm* serves as an allegory for the Russian Revolution and examines the degradation of revolutionary principles, whereas *1984* reveals the perils of dictatorship and pervasive surveillance. Notwithstanding censorship in certain nations, Orwell's writings have persisted, providing enduring admonitions against governmental authority and the repression of truth. These works illustrate how literature may function as a counternarrative, challenging the official historical account and governmental propaganda. Margaret Atwood's dystopian narrative *The Handmaid's Tale* attacks authoritarianism and sexism, illustrating a world in which women are oppressed by a theocratic state. Although situated in a fictional context, the novel addresses genuine political issues, including the regulation of women's bodies, the surveillance apparatus, and religious fanaticism. *The Handmaid's Tale* has emerged as a reference point for discourse on modern political matters, illustrating how literature may intricately mirror actual historical and political occurrences and reveal their inequities. James Baldwin's work *The Fire Next Time*, while essentially a compilation of essays, profoundly addresses the political challenges faced by African Americans throughout the civil rights movement. He attacks governmental authority and society's apathy towards racial injustice, arguing that literature bears the obligation to confront these matters. Baldwin's writing reflected the political realities of his era and significantly shaped public awareness of race relations in America. Pablo Neruda's epic poetry collection *Canto General* delineates the history of Latin America, emphasising the tribulations of indigenous populations, their mistreatment by colonial authorities, and the uprisings within the continent. His politically charged poetry faced censorship in Chile and other nations, yet it emerged as an appeal for unity for resistance forces. Neruda's works illustrate how writing may contest state repression, function as a counter-narrative to colonial history, and aid in the preservation of a literary heritage that represents the populace.

However, writing about politics is particularly difficult since, unlike music or movies, writing is a private activity. It can be difficult to adequately express the language or position of a group when working alone with only a computer and one's own hands and fingers. Fiction employs a distinct language that captures the subjective awareness of individuals, perceiving and understanding the world with moral uncertainty. Within this framework, different problems and desires constantly fluctuate and clash, ranging from unpleasant to pleasing, merging these two categories in enigmatic and unconventional manners that mirror the profound aspects of human nature through obscure and surreal reminders. We inhabit a realm characterised by extraordinary peculiarity and power, a realm that, despite our comprehension of it, remains incomprehensible. The world needs greater appreciation than we have demonstrated, as it is a realm governed by fundamental forces that influence our physical and mental states, as well as our societal systems.

In his essay *Why I Write*, George Orwell argues that the belief that art should be apart from politics is, in fact, a political stance in itself. Art is arguably the most noble of all human endeavours, which is why it requires protection. During times of crisis, artists must also be seen among those who guard, protect and preserve. Writers and intellectuals have to acknowledge that they cannot exist outside or separate themselves from the present moment and its demands. Whether they like it or not, they are confined inside the boundaries of their own generation and must operate within those limitations. Thinkers, regardless of whether they are considered public intellectuals or belong to the more reserved and less prominent category, have a primary responsibility to establish clear differences, especially in an era characterised by the thoughtless proliferation of moral equivalence.

Literature has numerous ways of representation. J.M. Coetzee, a white South African, expressed his opposition to the Apartheid state using a subtle and indirect approach, reminiscent of Platonic concepts, rather than engaging in overt political discourse. Coetzee argues that during periods of strong ideological influence, such as the present, when the coexistence of the novel and history is greatly limited, the novel has two choices: either to serve as a supplement or to engage in revolt. In contrast, Nadine Gordimer, a white South African writer who consistently opposed Apartheid, directly confronted political matters and used them to complement historical narratives in her literary works. Both of them were awarded the Nobel Prize for their contributions to writing about politics, demonstrating that there are multiple approaches to this subject. Gordimer supplemented politics in her work, while Coetzee rivalled it.

Is Kafka's work characterised by political themes? Does a spectrum exist to measure the level of political engagement of a writer or the political nature of specific literary themes? Alienation and outsiderness are prominent themes in Kafka's work. It is worth considering whether these themes stem from his identification as a despised minority residing among other marginalised groups or from his opposition to the imperial and royal Hapsburg authority. Conversely, are there any political elements included in Borges' stories? He strictly adheres to the concept of intellectual escapism through his distinctive literary metaphysics. What about Chekhov, whose remarkably skilful, character-focused portrayals appear, at first glance, to be devoid of political themes? Or Stefan Zweig, who endeavoured to maintain a neutral stance in all his fictional works, while also striving to establish a more refined and globally aware Europe in reality (and tragically took his own life due to despair caused by the Nazis in 1942)? Clearly, all of these writers were or are highly politically inclined.

All forms of art, including fiction, are inherently political. That remains valid even if the author refutes it or attempts to evade it. We have been advised to exercise caution in placing trust in the writer, but rather to place trust in the quality of their work. While this may appear to be a form of academic sophistry, it is particularly relevant when considering a writer who denies the principles of politics. It would be prudent to have this in mind. Art production is contingent upon the artist's freedom. The artist's commitment to freedom of speech is essential, as it is crucial for the preservation of a democratic society. Politics is an inescapable reality for writers and everyone else. We are all inevitably subject to the structures of authority and patterns of human conduct that encompass our lives. Choosing not to acknowledge or reject this just exposes one's inherent advantage.

In light of the above, therefore, whatever the circumstances, the writer community in Kashmir, particularly the emerging group of English-language authors, must remain committed to their craft and the literary tradition established by influential figures such as Agha Shahid Ali, Siddharth Gigoo, Mirza Waheed, Rahul Pandita, Basharat Peer, and many others. This fledgling tradition demands both integrity and resilience to flourish. Despite the divergence in narratives—whether between the Pandit and Muslim perspectives or among other sociopolitical and cultural divides—the literary tradition of Kashmir must thrive on its own terms, rooted in authenticity and originality. Writers must continue to explore and express the region's complexities, without bowing to external pressures or abandoning their creative integrity. Only through such dedication can this literary tradition grow, evolve, and offer a genuine reflection of the Kashmiri experience.

9

A Love Conversation in the Time of Quarantine

The sinking sun adorned itself with golden ornaments, its rays casting fleeting brilliance over loose clouds that seemed like hastily drawn maps of different nations. The scene caught my eye but failed to stir my heart. Beauty, after all, is a creation of the heart, not the eye, and my heart was burdened with the relentless sorrow of quarantine. This sorrow clung to me like an invisible shroud, a hovering darkness that overshadowed even the radiant clouds. My thoughts wandered until my friend's bitter analogy about his clumsy physique and the coronavirus seized my attention.

He lamented his unwholesome, ill-favoured appearance, recounting how no one spared him a glance during his two-mile walk through the bustling streets of his town. "I wish I were as famous—or infamous—as the coronavirus is now" he said with a wry smile. "Then I could intrude upon lives, claim attention, and occupy even the fairest of spaces. Or, at least, I wish I were as ubiquitous as the word 'quarantine,' for no other word has enjoyed such unprecedented prominence.

Even those who had never encountered it now wield it with ease and authority."

His words lingered, charged with the weight of irony and despair. Truly, what a powerful signifier it had become. Derrida's observation that the signified is slippery echoed in my mind, but here it seemed so explosive, dominating other meanings and forcing them into submission. Quarantine, a word once limited to the realm of public health, had now become a carrier of ideology, reshaping thoughts and emotions on a global scale.

When I glanced back at the sky, the luminous maps of clouds had dissolved into the encroaching darkness, leaving behind an empty vastness that mirrored the fear and uncertainty in my mind. These fears, fed by the virus and the isolation it imposed, seemed to alter my perception of everything familiar, warping the very fabric of reality. In an attempt to reclaim some semblance of comfort, I slammed the window shut as if to barricade the encroaching void. I picked up my phone, my tether to a distant sense of connection, and reached out to my beloved, whose voice, though physically distant, was a solace amidst the unsettling vastness of quarantine.

Me: Hello, hope you're finished with washing your hands?

She: Oh, I was busy making a homemade sanitizer. Now I can wash my hands to absolute satisfaction. It lathers beautifully. I rinse and rinse until, as they say, the fat membrane of the invisible virus dissolves into nothingness.

Me: But what if the virus isn't on your hands at all?

She: How can I ever know it's not there?

Me: Suppose someone tells you the virus is in your brain. Would you rinse your brain too?

She: How can this little, insignificant thing reach my brain when I've already rinsed it to death on my hands?

Me: Little insignificant thing? Really?

She: Well, now it might appear larger than life itself. But ultimately, it's still a little, insignificant thing.

Me: No, it's a little, insignificant thing, but one that's become larger than the world itself.

She: Does it matter what we think? It is what it is.

Me: If opinions don't matter, why should we bother forming them? We aren't just quarantined in body; our minds are quarantined too. The virus has infected our thoughts, caging them within its shadow. It's become impossible to think of anything else.

She: Shut up and listen. Do you know what haunts me after I'm done washing my hands? I can't bring myself to turn off the running tap, fearing I'll catch the virus from it. I leave it running and call my mother to turn it off. I barely touch door knobs. I've started using my feet more than my hands.

Me: But what if your mother catches the virus from the tap? Don't you think she might spread it to the whole family?

She: I keep physical distance from everyone. I just hope she never catches it from the tap.

Me: But why on earth are we talking about all this? I was feeling heart-sore. I thought you would comfort me like you did that hot summer afternoon on a houseboat. Your voice, deep and hushed like the cold breeze rising from the heaving Dal Lake, promised me a beautiful world, a home I have fancied ever since.

She: Oh, you are so naive, aren't you? In the time of quarantine, a mask or a sanitizer is more important than love. No vague ruminations on love, please. Even the fondest memories of love can't shield you from the indomitable fear of this virus breaking into your mind.

Me: How is that possible? What about our love—the love you always called pure and ideal? Surely, your love must still be more important than any sanitizer in the world?

She: I don't mean I have forgotten our love. It's just that I have postponed the idea. The whole world has come to a grinding halt, and you still grumble about love. This is the time of quarantine. Everything else can wait—not just your love, but perhaps even God.

Me: Great God! What about all those words of ideal love you whispered into my ear? Didn't I tell you, on all such occasions, that your warm breath moistened the barren ridges of my ear? Those moments melted the entire history of sublime musings on love into the reality of our bodies. How can this petty event reduce the grandeur of our love to a sanitizer or a face mask?

She: See, I'm going to wash my hands. I don't have time for these frivolous things. All I know is that this quarantine is the only antidote to the pandemic. It's the only thing that can preserve our bodies for any future transactions of love.

Me: But you told me once that love is like a transcendental signified upon which we build the meaning of our lives. You said it was constant and steadfast, like the northern star. If you remember, you also said our bodies are just another form of matter, while love is the life and spirit animating it. Now I'm afraid you'll deny the relevance of the body in love itself.

She: It's time to revisit general perceptions about the body. By the way, I didn't invite this pandemic to earth. It may have deferred or postponed everything, but I hope that, in time, everything—including your body and love—will be restored.

Me: But my body needs it now. My body is my perception of love. Without my body, my perception of love ceases to exist. And ideal love can't be subjected to or made vulnerable by any eventuality, no matter how dreary or decimating.

She: Actually, I don't know much about love. But I do know about the sublime complexity of the body. Love must be just a fragment of that complexity. I don't need your body in love right now because I can't put the entirety of that complexity at risk for just one fragment of it.

Me: Then what about all those great books written in praise of ideal love?

She: I haven't written any of those great books. Go and find their authors. Ask them how it feels in the time of quarantine.

Me: But why are we talking about all this? I just wanted you to comfort me.

She: Then wash your hands, and don't forget to rinse hard. I'm going to wash mine.

She left the conversation. Meanwhile, a gruff male voice hollered through the mosque loudspeaker, "Our village has been declared a red zone. The movement of people is strictly prohibited. Stay home, stay safe." The voice disturbed the poor villagers as if it had just announced the apocalypse or the arrival of a tsunami.

Angrily, I pushed aside a book on metaphysics lying before me and began contemplating the importance of a sanitizer in the time of quarantine.

10

BETWEEN THE TEXT AND THE READER: A DEATH IN CONTEXT

Ali Chak passed away the other morning, a death as sudden as it was shrouded in speculation. He had just returned from the mosque after attending the early morning prayers, his breath mingling with the densest fog of the season. Moments after stepping into the warmth of his home, his wife had asked him for tea. He had barely settled on his bed before his life ebbed away.

By the time the news spread, a river of people had flooded his home. Grief hung thick in the air as his wife cried, "He never complained of anything—nothing at all!" Her voice cracked, echoing her disbelief.

I stood there, stunned, as the house filled with murmurs and movement. What began as quiet condolences quickly turned into a cacophony of theories.

"It must be a cardiac arrest," someone asserted with conviction.

"No, no, it's a brain haemorrhage," argued another, shaking his head as though dismissing all other possibilities.

While I nudged my way through the ever-thickening crowd, the voices grew louder, and more animated, each person offering a new explanation for Ali Chak's sudden demise.

"He always said the cold never bothered him," an old man declared, shaking his fist as if in accusation. "He'd walk around in summer clothes even in this bone-chilling winter. It has to be hypothermia!"

Someone else shifted the blame, eyes narrowing as they pointed fingers at his elder son. "It's his carelessness—always leaving his father to fend for himself in this weather!"

And then, a whisper, almost conspiratorial, rose above the din. "No, no, it's black magic. The younger son... he's been casting spells, everyone knows!"

The house had transformed into a theatre of interpretations, each version more fractured, more surreal than the last. In the heart of that foggy morning, Ali Chak's death had become less of a tragedy and more of a canvas for speculation—a fragmented story pieced together by a crowd desperate for answers.

I wondered if the buzz was fuelled more by the fear and mystique of death itself or by the sheer suddenness of Ali Chak's passing. What intrigued me most was my own response—was I more startled by his untimely death or by the swirling tide of interpretations it provoked?

In that moment, I was reminded of the endlessly shifting debates in academia about the existence and meaning of a "text." Roland Barthes' concept of a text as a "multidimensional space" came to mind—a site where discursive elements blend, clash, and regenerate in infinite combinations. Chak's death, much like a text in Barthesian terms, had given rise to a myriad of interpretations.

Each explanation—whether rooted in medical science, superstition, familial blame, or personal bias—was revealing in its own way. These interpretations were at once individual and collective, cultural or community-centric, mutually antagonistic yet interconnected. Together, they formed a vast domain of meaning, expanding outward like ripples in a pond, each one inviting yet another layer of interpretation—much like the ever-expanding nature of the universe itself.

This collective interpretive act reminded me of the American literary critic Jonathan Culler's idea of the "system of signs," where meaning is not intrinsic but relational, constructed through a web of cultural codes and shared understandings. In this sense, the varied reactions to Chak's death were not just responses to a singular event but manifestations of a larger collective consciousness—a system within which we all exist, and outside of which it is nearly impossible to imagine meaning.

Chak's death, then, was not just an end; it became a narrative, a text, a space for meaning-making where the act of interpretation was as revealing as the event itself.

The point here is that interpreting a text is an inherently complex process, involving a multitude of factors working simultaneously. It is never simply about the text as a fixed repository of meaning, nor can it be reduced to reader response alone. Interpretation cannot be confined to history, the present, or the future, nor can it be limited to language in isolation. Instead, it emerges as a dynamic admixture of all these elements, as vividly illustrated by the varied and layered explanations surrounding Chak's death.

Stanley Fish's concept of "Interpretive Communities" provides valuable insight into this process. These communities exist beyond just the text and the reader, actively participating in the construction of meaning. They don't merely "construe" a text; they also "construct" new meanings, shaped by shared cultural, historical, and social frameworks.

This meaning-making process, however, is far from straightforward. It is imperceptibly governed by other sets of texts, interpretations, and frameworks, each shaped in turn by yet another layer of meanings. It is a recursive and interconnected practice, where interpretation feeds upon interpretation, creating an intricate web of meanings that continuously evolves.

While interpretation is fundamentally a communal activity, this does not preclude it from being individual or psychological. On the contrary, individual insights and psychological dimensions enrich the collective process, adding depth and diversity to the interpretive act. In this sense, interpretation is both deeply personal and communal—a synthesis of the many forces that shape how we understand and assign meaning to the world around us. This is where Roland Barthes becomes particularly relevant. In his celebrated essay, *The Death of the Author*, Barthes shifts the focus from the role of interpretive communities to that of the individual reader. For Barthes, the author is merely the "origin" of the text—a figure whose significance diminishes once the text is created. The reader, on the other hand, is the "destination," the one who brings the text to life through interpretation. In the case of Chak's death, some people attributing it to his sons' carelessness or accusations of magic represent psychological responses detached from the "origin"—the actual event of his death. These interpretations reflect the individual's subjective fears, biases, and cultural contexts rather than an objective account of what occurred. However, Barthes' emphasis on the reader does not suggest that these interpretations are the most authentic or final. Readers' responses are subtly influenced and shaped by other interpretations, deeply embedded in the cultural, historical, and social settings shared by both the reader and the text.

Moreover, the act of interpretation involves bridging the gaps between the origin (the text) and the reader. Wolfgang Iser, in *The Act of Reading*, describes these gaps as spaces within the textual structure that require the reader's imagination and insight to fill. He introduces the concept of the "implied reader," who interacts with the text, exploring and filling in these blanks to produce meaning. This differs from Barthes' focus on the reader and Fish's interpretive communities, yet it is equally valid in highlighting the dynamic nature of interpretation. In the case of Chak's death, the gaps—the absence of concrete causes—invite interpretations such as hypothermia or his perceived carelessness in not dressing warmly enough for winter. Iser describes this as an interactive relationship between the author (or origin) and the reader, where the author provides the "artistic" framework and the reader completes the "aesthetic" realization. Interpretation, then, is not just a passive reception of meaning but an active process, one where the individual reader, the community, and the gaps within the text all work together to construct a multifaceted understanding.

Chak's death becomes more than a singular event—it transforms into a textual phenomenon, where every interpretation enriches and complicates the narrative, illustrating the profound complexity of meaning-making itself.

There are other possible causes of interpretation beyond those already discussed. One influential perspective comes from Jacques Derrida, who argues that a text is inherently unstable and open to endless interpretations. In his view, the inherent discursiveness of a text creates doubt and stimulates greater interpretative activity by the reader. This idea is deeply rooted in Derrida's concept of différance, introduced in his seminal work *Of Grammatology*. According to Derrida, a text is not a fixed entity but a dynamic space where "traces of differences" interact, constantly deferring meaning. Ali Chak, as a figure, wasn't a singular or static entity either. His character embodied a diversity of contradictory traits, making it impossible for him to dictate or control the varied responses to his death. These interpretations arise not merely because of the ambiguity surrounding the event but also due to the inherent fluidity and multiplicity within the text (or event) itself, as Derrida suggests.

However, while textual fluidity plays a significant role in shaping interpretations, it would be reductive to ignore the influence of historical context. Those offering opinions about Chak's death inevitably draw upon their prior knowledge of him and his past, unconsciously connecting it to the present occurrence. A text, therefore, cannot be fully interpreted solely within its inherent discursiveness. Hans-Georg Gadamer's hermeneutics sheds light on this interplay between past and present through his concept of the "fusion of horizons." Gadamer argues that understanding—or interpretation—is a "historically effected event," shaped by the interplay of past events and the present understanding of the reader. This, however, does not negate the text's active role in the production of meaning. Umberto Eco, in his seminal work *The Open Work*, emphasizes that texts themselves guide reader responses in two ways: as an "interpretation" and as a "performance." Eco posits that while the reader plays a crucial role in constructing meaning, the text provides a framework that channels these interpretations, offering possibilities while maintaining certain boundaries. In the context of Chak's death, the interpretations are informed by both the inherent ambiguities of the event (its textual fluidity) and the historical context of Chak's life, filtered through the readers' horizons. The text, as Derrida, Gadamer, and Eco collectively imply, is neither wholly self-contained nor entirely subject to external forces. Instead, it exists in a dynamic, collaborative space where meaning is continuously constructed and reconstructed. This process highlights the dance between the text's discursiveness, its historical grounding, and the reader's active participation in the act of interpretation.

Moreover, the responses to Chak's death also reveal the positionality of those making the interpretations. These individuals know him, belong to the same social and cultural milieu, and thus possess the authority—or the "edge"—to articulate their views in a way that outsiders might not. This brings Michel Foucault into the discussion, particularly his assertion that knowledge is "not for knowing," but for "cutting." For Foucault, knowledge is intrinsically linked to power—it does not simply aim to counter arguments but seeks to organize and establish control. In this sense, the responses to Chak's death are not just expressions of grief or speculation; they also serve to assert the speakers' positions of authority within their community, shaping the narrative according to their social and cultural capital.

Another critical factor shaping interpretation is the material conditions of the interpreters themselves. In Chak's case, the responses reflect not only cultural norms but also the class, financial conditions, and ignorance of those responding. These material realities inform the lens through which they interpret his death, revealing as much about the interpreters as the event itself. Here, Terry Eagleton's views on textual interpretation become highly relevant. Eagleton argues that there is no such thing as "a purely literary reading," as every interpretation is shaped by the socio-economic and material conditions of the reader. While a text may foreground certain elements, it inevitably obscures or sidelines others, creating a space for class, ideology, and material realities to influence the interpretive process.

Ultimately, no single approach to interpretation can claim to hold the complete truth or provide the final word on a text. Similarly, no single interpretation can fully encompass the multiplicity of meanings that a text—or an event like Chak's death—might generate. Beyond the frameworks discussed—those of Barthes, Derrida, Gadamer, Eco, Foucault, and Eagleton—there are countless other factors, both tangible and intangible, that contribute to meaning-making.

These theoretical approaches are valuable as they help identify significant forces at play in the interpretive process. However, a text remains perpetually open to interpretation, resisting closure or definitive meaning. This openness ensures that the act of interpretation continues to evolve, shaped by the dynamic interplay of the text, the reader, the community, and the material realities that frame their interaction. It is in this fluidity that the true richness of interpretation lies.

References

Barthes, Roland. "The Death of the Author." *Image-Music-Text*. Translated by Stephen Heath, Hill and Wang, 1977, pp. 142-148.

Derrida, Jacques. *Of Grammatology*. Translated by Gayatri Chakravorty Spivak, Johns Hopkins University Press, 1976.

Eagleton, Terry. *Literary Theory: An Introduction*. Blackwell, 1983.

Eco, Umberto. *The Open Work*. Translated by Anna Cancogni, Harvard University Press, 1989.

Foucault, Michel. *The Archaeology of Knowledge*. Translated by A.M. Sheridan Smith, Pantheon Books, 1972.

Gadamer, Hans-Georg. *Truth and Method*. Translated by Joel Weinsheimer and Donald G. Marshall, 2nd ed., Continuum, 1994.

Iser, Wolfgang. *The Act of Reading: A Theory of Aesthetic Response*. Johns Hopkins University Press, 1978.

11

BINARIES IN CRISIS: KASHMIR, JOURNALISM, AND THE STRUGGLE FOR TRUTH

As a society, we humans both consciously and unconsciously rely on an expansive, pre-existing cultural repertoire of knowledge to create meaning. The act of meaning-making is only possible when we temporarily halt the otherwise continuous and elusive flow of signification. It is through the complex cohesion within the deferral of absolute connotations of signs that our collective behaviour and norms are both enabled and constrained. Each idea or discursive formation in this repertoire carries with it a memory or history, which supports its existence within the system. However, long after the idea has shed its history and memory, it assumes the appearance of naturalness—a subtle, silent process where nature replaces history. Nowhere is this shift more evident than in the cultural performance of deeply entrenched, mutually antagonistic binaries. For instance, the connotative significance of the term 'white' not only creates a problematic of inclusion and exclusion but also assigns us specific roles. However, my focus here is not on the formation of these binaries, but on the fluid and interchangeable nature of their connotations. I think that, due to the inevitable imbalance in power relations, the fixed meanings of binaries can undergo a transformation at any time. For example, the binary between the civilized and the uncivilized or truth and untruth can challenge their historically assumed meanings. We have seen 'regimes of truth' in different cultures turn into 'regimes of untruth,' and the normalisation of 'evil' has, at times, allowed it to replace its binary counterpart, 'good,' leaving little to no room for clear categorisation.

Now, let us examine the present condition of journalism in Kashmir in light of the argument above. Kashmir, much like Barthes' myth and Althusser's problematic, is an organized body of knowledge primarily defined by its tumultuous political history and present. The pervasive influence of the political has deeply infiltrated our culture, shaping it to its core. Its overt 'repressive hierarchy' has normalised capitulation as a collective response, intruding into the very fabric of our social behaviour. The *parole* of our current political despair is largely shaped by the *langue* of our contentious political past. Within the confines of this *langue* and *parole*, we have witnessed a persistent battle between the binaries of truth and untruth. Yet, we may have overlooked the point where these binaries begin to overlap at the connotative level, subtly reversing their traditional roles and consumption in practice.

Let us turn our attention to the case of Kashmiri journalists such as Gowher Geelani, Masrat Zahra, and Peerzada Ashiq, who have faced intimidation, harassment, and detention for their journalistic endeavours. Within the complex political and cultural context of Kashmir, their voices represent the embodiment of truth. Drawing from the pre-existing cultural repertoire of knowledge, these journalists attempt to highlight and foreground a domain where truth can assert its dominance over its binary opposite, 'untruth,' much like the long-standing tradition of binaries across different cultures. One of the most notable and successful efforts to foreground this domain has been recognised globally, as evidenced by Kashmiri photojournalists winning the prestigious Pulitzer Prize. These journalists, when they speak or demonstrate, refer not merely to theoretical abstractions but to the lived reality of a cultural mechanism—a system of metonymic cultural codes that, in practice, shape the very 'truth' of our existence. In this sense, their work represents a form of truth for the regional majority; it is not an unfounded, speculative meditation, but a truth that is directly linked to the way we live and experience the world.

However, the opposing binary of 'untruth,' as represented by the overbearing political machinery, is not content to remain static in its position of power. This binary, entrenched in the official narrative, refuses to be relegated forever to a weaker, subjugated position. In the complex system of signification, the supposed 'weaker' binary—untruth—has the power to challenge and even overturn the 'privileged' binary of truth, causing a shift in the prevailing cultural dynamics. This shift does not simply involve the deferral of binaries, but their interchange, with each binary swapping positions in a fluid manner that reflects the ongoing cultural contestation. The 'truth,' as envisioned by the dedicated journalists, is countered by the political apparatus that devalues it, relegating it to a position of 'unlawfulness,' branding it as 'glorifying terrorism,' or accusing it of being 'prejudicial to national integrity' or 'causing disaffection against the country.' In invoking the immediate binary of 'national' and 'anti-national,' the government seeks to destabilise the definitional solidity of 'truth,' undermining it by elevating the opposite— 'untruth'—to a privileged position.

As this countering process unfolds, the binaries not only swap positions but also reshape the structure of cultural practices. The contestation between these binaries is not a mere theoretical exercise; it is a power struggle that, in the case of Kashmir, leads to the panoptic establishment of 'untruth' as the dominant and privileged binary. Over time, this contestation has the potential to obscure the lines between history and nature, blurring the distinction between the lived political experience and the naturalised ideological narrative. This phenomenon can be likened to the experience of a government employee who initially finds it difficult to adhere to stringent rules and policies. Over time, however, under the weight of constant subjection to these rules, the employee begins to internalise and live by them. Eventually, the employee does not merely follow the rules but becomes an embodiment of them, so much so that the process of compliance becomes so silent and subtle that the individual begins to mistake the rules for something inherent and natural. This naturalisation of the ideological becomes a process so ingrained that, at some point, it becomes nearly impossible to distinguish between what is historically constructed and what is mistakenly perceived as a natural, unchangeable truth.

In this way, the contestation of binaries in Kashmir— where the opposing forces of truth and untruth dynamically interact—leads to a profound reshaping of cultural and political practices, ultimately influencing the way we perceive reality and, more crucially, how we come to accept certain ideologies as inevitable and natural.

However, this seemingly debilitating function of binaries should not be viewed as something that merely suspends or sabotages reality. In fact, the ongoing interplay of these binaries is productive in its own right. It continually opens up new possibilities for understanding and engaging with reality, allowing for a dynamic exploration of different perspectives and interpretations. Moreover, this constant shifting of binaries provides valuable insights into how the complex process of meaning-making operates across cultures. The interplay of these binary oppositions not only exposes the fluidity of signification but also highlights how meanings are deferred, negotiated, and constructed in real-world contexts.

Even in a system where voices are marginalised or suppressed, this process remains a critical site of potential for cultural and political resistance. No matter how skillfully the panoptic forces of power attempt to silence dissent or relegate certain voices to an unprivileged binary, those voices continue to persist within the broader, ever-evolving system of signification. This is where the true resilience of marginalised voices lies: in their capacity to exist and find relevance within a vast, interconnected cultural system that transcends immediate repression. The awarding of the Pulitzer Prize to Kashmiri photojournalists is a testament to this enduring existence. It is not just a recognition of their work, but also a confirmation that even in the face of severe control, the voice of truth and resistance is capable of breaking through, and finding its place in the cultural dialogue.

12

CONTEXTUALIZING THE BOIS LOCKER ROOM SCANDAL

Our understanding of ourselves—our identities, bodies, relationships, and behaviours—is intricately shaped by an invisible yet pervasive system of rules that govern us on both conscious and unconscious levels. This system of rules, much like the rules that regulate a cricketer's performance within the boundaries of a sport, dictates how we perceive, engage with, and express our social selves. In the case of cricket, for example, the rules not only provide the framework for the game but also carve out the identity of the cricketer. When a player transgresses these rules—whether through poor conduct, misconduct, or unethical behaviour—the sport doesn't just penalise them; it challenges the very essence of their identity as a player, forcing them into a space of reflection, recalibration, and, often, punishment. This disciplinary mechanism works to restore the individual to a state of "normalcy," or conformity with the accepted standards of the sport.

However, the rules within any given domain—whether in sports, society, or culture—are not static. They evolve, shift, and transform over time in response to changing circumstances, ideologies, and power structures. This dynamic process, as we see in the realm of sport, directly impacts the identity, performance or behaviour of participants, as what was once acceptable or normalised might no longer be so, requiring individuals to adapt or face exclusion. Society at large functions in a similar manner. The ways we interpret our roles, relationships, and behaviours are governed by an ever-changing system of societal rules and norms. These norms are not only informed by major cultural institutions like religion, law, or government but are also shaped by less formal sources, such as social networks, popular culture, and media. Together, these complex networks of rules intertwine and influence our perceptions of concepts like body, gender, and sexuality.

Take, for example, how our understanding of sex and the body is not a static truth but rather a discursive formation influenced by a host of institutions, from religion to medicine, law, and social media. Each of these institutions contributes to defining, constraining, and, at times, expanding what we consider normal or acceptable when it comes to issues of the body and sexuality. But as these societal constructs evolve, so too does our perception of the body, sex, and relationships, reflecting broader shifts in our collective consciousness. In this sense, these evolving rules shape not just individual identity but collective norms, enforcing certain behaviours while questioning or punishing others. This intersection of changing rules and evolving perceptions provides the context in which events such as the Bois Locker Room scandal emerge, highlighting the clash between old and new norms, and questioning the adequacy of current societal mechanisms to address behaviour that straddles both public and private spaces. To understand the Bois Locker Room incident, we must first explore the complex and evolving cultural perceptions surrounding body and sex in India. The discomfort and repression around these topics are deeply ingrained in Indian society, shaped by centuries of religious, moral, and legal discourses. Historically, we do not fully "own" our bodies in a natural, unmediated sense. Instead, our inclinations—be it sexual or bodily—are often meticulously controlled, suppressed, and redirected by societal rules and expectations. This process is akin to mowing the grass when it grows beyond a desired size. In certain cultures, these inclinations might be allowed more freedom of expression, but Indian society has generally been sensitive, constrained, and reluctant to fully acknowledge the natural desires of the body.

This constraint is not just external but also internalised. The discourses around body, sex, and desire in Indian society are overwhelmingly shaped by religious, legal, and philosophical perspectives that position these subjects as private, forbidden, or shameful. From an early age, individuals are taught to view the body and sex as topics to be avoided, repressed, and even disowned. It's not uncommon for even the most educated individuals to remain silent or avoid discussions around body and sex, despite being well-versed in a range of other subjects. This silence becomes not only a personal choice but a cultural norm, reflecting how society has internalised an estrangement from its own natural state.

Furthermore, this repression is not just about silence—it is about the deep moralising of bodily functions. Society has conditioned itself to associate body parts and sexual desires with notions of filth, vulgarity, and impurity. A simple touch of what is deemed 'dirty' (such as genitalia) triggers an instinctive need to wash hands, a physical manifestation of the cultural disgust ingrained in us. These practices speak to a larger pattern of alienation, where the body and its desires are treated as foreign, separate from the self. This alienation extends into language, where, despite the power of words to shape our perceptions and actions, both body and sex are deliberately avoided in everyday conversation, replaced with euphemisms, ambiguities, or complete silence.

The Bois Locker Room scandal, which revealed conversations of young men objectifying women and discussing sexually explicit topics in a dehumanising way, becomes a reflection of these cultural tensions. It exposes the deeply embedded contradictions within Indian society: while the body and sex are repressed and sanitised in public discourse, their suppression leads to their perversion in private spaces. The scandal serves as a reminder of how the historical repression of sexual expression can give rise to harmful behaviours, such as misogyny, objectification, and a lack of empathy towards others. In essence, the incident reveals the consequences of alienating the body and desire: the emergence of a toxic culture where repressed emotions and desires are channelled into unhealthy expressions, ultimately undermining the very purpose of healthy sexual discourse.

The stark contrast between the cultural silence surrounding sex and the crude, violent expressions that arise in its absence suggests the need for a shift in how society engages with these topics. It is not enough to simply demand repression or silence; the body and sex must be acknowledged and understood in a way that promotes respect, consent, and healthy expression. Only by re-examining and recalibrating our cultural perceptions of the body and sexuality can we hope to prevent incidents like the Bois Locker Room scandal from becoming normalised or ignored in future.

The Bois Locker Room scandal, however, reveals a deeper, more gradual transformation that has been occurring within social structures and human behaviour—one that has been slow, almost imperceptible, but undeniably profound. This transformation is not entirely a result of cultural erosion but rather reflects a shifting, almost inevitable, reconfiguration of cultural norms under the influence of rapid technological progress. Much like how technology has revolutionized other spheres of life, its impact on cultural perceptions of body and sex has been far-reaching, and the speed of this shift has mirrored the unprecedented pace of technological advancements in recent years.

The societal disciplinary mechanisms, traditionally rigid in their efforts to uphold moralistic norms, have been more accommodating to these technological changes, recognizing the economic potential and benefits they offer. While this accommodation has spurred advancements in various fields, it has also altered fundamental aspects of human interaction and perception. This change has particularly affected urban spaces, where technology and the forces of globalisation have had a stronger presence. Metropolitan cities have become hotbeds for these cultural fissures, especially among the younger generation, who are more disconnected from traditional cultural inhibitions about body and sex. The hyper-connectedness of today's world, along with access to information and communication technologies, has provided this generation with an unfiltered, often unmediated, window into different cultures and ways of living, which can clash with the more conservative attitudes that prevail in Indian society.

In light of this, the Bois Locker Room scandal should not be seen as a sudden shock or an anomaly but rather as the culmination of a cultural shift that was already underway. This shift has been accelerated by the pervasive exposure to foreign cultures and values, facilitated by technology. Online platforms, especially social media, have become a breeding ground for changing ideas about body and sex. The availability of explicit content, the normalisation of objectification and commercialisation of the body, and the growing acceptance of previously stigmatised bodily expressions have significantly shifted perceptions. Sexuality is increasingly viewed as something more liberated, more commodified, and more visible in everyday life—something as commonplace and accessible as the act of washing one's hands.

The increasing accessibility to online pornography, sexual content, and even medical solutions for sexual health has slowly detached the body from the cultural baggage of repression. Instead, the body is increasingly perceived as a more autonomous entity, one that is free to express, display, and consume desires without the restraint of the traditional taboos that once controlled such expressions. This shift, however, comes with its own set of complications. As body and sex move from the private, hidden realm to the more open and public sphere, the lack of a cultural framework for navigating this transformation can create a vacuum that is filled with distorted expressions of sexuality, such as those witnessed in the Bois Locker Room incident.

At the same time, the growing class inequality, changing gender dynamics in the workplace, and the increasing ease with which individuals can access information have further exacerbated these cultural tensions. As the divide between the privileged and the marginalised continues to widen, this cultural shift manifests in dangerous ways, especially among young people who, for the first time, are grappling with new forms of sexual expression without fully understanding the power dynamics, ethical considerations, and respect for boundaries that ought to accompany them. This lack of understanding, coupled with an environment of anonymity provided by digital platforms, has led to the commodification of women and the dehumanisation of their bodies, as seen in the disturbing discussions that took place within the Bois Locker Room group.

In essence, the incident represents a cultural crossroads. While it is a manifestation of the changing perceptions about body and sex, it also underscores the need for a more nuanced, ethical approach to the evolving discourse surrounding these topics. The challenge lies not in condemning these changes but in addressing the void they leave behind—how to balance liberation with responsibility, openness with respect, and freedom with consent. The growing normalisation of body and sex should be accompanied by a cultural education that fosters empathy, consent, and healthy relationships, ensuring that the transformation occurring in the public sphere does not lead to further objectification, harm, or violence.

For the young school-going teens involved in the infamous Bois Locker Room chat, the body has ceased to be a private realm, a space of modesty or something to be hidden away. Instead, it has become just another easily accessible object for ridicule, manipulation, and entertainment. The body, once cloaked in enforced repression and morally charged taboos, is now increasingly losing its former cultural significance. These historical associations—where the body was linked with shame, secrecy, or guilt—are rapidly losing relevance in the face of an emerging cultural shift that treats the body as a commodity or spectacle. The scandalous conversations that erupted in the Bois Locker Room reflect this transformation; what was once considered a base, shameful bodily instinct is now more openly embraced and redefined as the purity of desire.

This change has seeped into mainstream culture, where the body is no longer seen as a private mystery but as a visible, public entity. Sex, once perceived as something confined to certain categories of people, has now become an omnipresent feature of modern life, widely accessible and openly discussed. In this new cultural landscape, the boundaries surrounding the body and sexuality are shifting, and this cultural liberation is not confined to a single gender or group. Even feminist critiques of the incident, which emphasize the objectification of the female body, miss the mark to some extent. This is because the female body, like its male counterpart, is also being subjected to this broader, collectivistic cultural change. The body has, in a sense, become an object for consumption and display, transforming the cultural fabric in ways that challenge traditional norms.

Exposure to pornography, explicit imagery, and sexualized films has significantly altered the sanctity once ascribed to both the body and the institution of marriage. What was once held as sacred and private—such as the marital relationship— has been destabilised by the pervasive presence of sexual content in everyday life. This phenomenon can be understood as a gradual, though radical, rupture of a previously repressed collective unconscious. The slow but inevitable dismantling of traditional boundaries around body and sex has opened up new spaces for expression, but it also comes with unintended consequences. Calling this shift merely a matter of moral decay, legal transgression, or unchecked patriarchy does not address the deeper cultural roots of the change.

What remains clear, however, is that as long as the objectification of the body and the commercialisation of sex does not pose a direct threat to the economic interests that drive the dominant power structures, this cultural shift will persist and even intensify. The governing mechanisms of society have long since adapted to the commercialisation of sexuality, given the economic benefits it generates. Whether through the sale of sexualised imagery, the booming pornography industry, or the commodification of bodies in media and advertising, the economic logic of this transformation is too powerful to easily constrain. Until these forces are directly challenged or disrupted by a broader, more radical cultural shift, the growing normalisation of sexualised bodies and desires will continue to define modern cultural identity.

13

CORONAVIRUS: THE UNFOLDING OF AN EPISTEMIC CRISIS

Epistemology, the philosophical study of knowledge, examines the nature, formation, and justification of beliefs, as well as their relationship to truth. This complex process of belief formation and internalisation often operates below the threshold of conscious awareness, making it nearly imperceptible. Over time, these beliefs solidify into deeply rooted traditions, shaping societal and individual ontologies. Given the layered history of these processes, an abrupt disruption of these entrenched epistemological structures seems improbable. The "unbecoming" of these beliefs—the process of questioning and dismantling them—often mirrors the gradual nature of their formation. However, extraordinary events, such as the coronavirus pandemic, represent a "black swan" phenomenon that disrupts the status quo. While such events may not entirely dismantle our structured systems of beliefs and values, they compel us to critically re-evaluate the relevance of prevailing ideologies, institutions, and human behaviours, potentially reshaping our collective epistemic foundations.

The relentless coronavirus pandemic has caused unprecedented disruption across the globe. Confused world leaders addressing their nations, a media frenzy advocating stricter control and preventive measures, the hyperbolic reactions on social media, and the lockdown of towns, cities, and vital centers of business and education all underscore the magnitude of this crisis. While the pandemic poses an immediate threat to life, starkly highlighting humanity's otherwise normalised uncertainty about death, it also diverts attention from a deeper disruption. The virus challenges the perceived relevance and truthfulness of long-standing behaviours, beliefs, and the supposedly robust institutions that underpin global society, institutions that have evolved quietly alongside human life. Though this pandemic is unlikely to annihilate humanity entirely, it serves as a stark reminder of the vulnerabilities in our social fabric. It urges us to learn critical lessons, particularly the need to reconstruct societal structures with greater foresight, resilience, and preparedness to tackle future crises more effectively.

Let us begin by examining the ideology that drives our economic system and how it has been run roughshod by the coronavirus pandemic. As the crisis deepens, the roof of our economic structure is collapsing under the weight of its foundational ideology: capitalism. While health experts urge people to stay home to prevent the spread of the virus, this advice exposes the stark inequities of the system. The working class, unlike the super-wealthy who can retreat to germ-free sanctuaries on private jets, cannot afford the luxury of staying home. For them, the choice is harrowing: risk exposure to the virus or fall victim to the equally merciless "virus" of hunger.

This system of compulsion forces workers to rise from their beds, use crowded public transport, and labour in unsafe environments, perpetuating a cycle that sustains both their survival and the economic mechanism.

Even healthcare, a basic necessity, remains inaccessible to many. The looming question of how patients might be saddled with exorbitant bills for a still-awaited coronavirus vaccine highlights the structural flaws of a profit-driven medical system. Kate Pickett and Richard Wilkinson, in their book *The Spirit Level: Why Greater Equality Makes Societies Stronger*, argue that wealth and power inequalities create a state of chronic stress. This stress wreaks havoc on bodily systems, such as the cardiovascular and immune systems, leaving individuals more vulnerable to health problems.

The current crisis underscores the urgent need to rethink and rebuild our societal structures. The solution lies not in a utopian liberal system providing temporary free medical care but in a complete overhaul of our priorities. A reimagined society must place human needs—not profit—at the core of its production processes. In such a system, healthcare would no longer bc dictated by the profit motives of wealthy capitalists controlling hospitals, pharmaceutical companies, and insurance systems. This moment of reckoning deconstructs the capitalist ideologies of market mechanisms that have entrenched themselves in the modern age of radical nationalism. It is a call to envision a society driven by equity, resilience, and collective well-being.

Secondly, let us examine how the novel coronavirus has the potential to redefine the semantics of nationalism. In India, nationalism often transcends its political roots to become a quasi-religious sentiment. Unfortunately, this sentiment has long been confined to an obsession with territorial borders and the imagined valour of soldiers perpetually sacrificing their lives to defend them. The pandemic, however, offers an opportunity to reorient this deeply ingrained notion of patriotism. In these challenging times, our patriotic feelings should shift away from glorifying militaristic endeavours and instead celebrate the contributions of doctors, nurses, pharmacists, volunteers, and utility workers. These individuals risk their lives daily to protect and heal others, embodying a form of service far more profound and immediate than any imaginary war. Their unflinching dedication to preserving life and ensuring societal functioning represents the truest form of devotion to the nation.

The coronavirus pandemic thus presents an opportunity to redefine nationalism as a sentiment rooted in nurturing life and safeguarding the health and well-being of a nation's people. It challenges us to view patriotism not as a tool for opposing or threatening other nations, but as a collective effort to build a healthier, more resilient society. In doing so, it shifts the focus of nationalism from territoriality and conflict to solidarity and care.

Another critical lesson that the coronavirus pandemic offers is the need to reassess the overbearing influence of certain religious teachings in shaping our sociological imagination. Historically, religion has not only endured adverse events—such as epidemics, disasters, wars, and displacements—but has also been quick to issue emphatic judgments about these occurrences. In underdeveloped and developing nations, where healthcare systems are already ill-equipped to combat a crisis of this magnitude, the dominance of what Milan Kundera calls "sacrosanct certainties" often exacerbates the problem. For instance, some communities promote unscientific remedies like cow urine or dung as antidotes to the virus, while others claim divine immunity as members of a "chosen few." Such attitudes, rooted in celestial approval and misplaced superiority, not only disavow the realities of the virus but also foster dangerous complacency. In extreme cases, some even sadistically attribute the suffering of others to divine retribution for perceived irreligiosity or nonconformity to their faith.

In these times of global quarantine and crisis, it is imperative for religions to confront and discard obsolete beliefs and practices that hinder public health efforts. It must be recognised that the coronavirus does not discriminate based on religious affiliation or piety. While teachings like "namaste" or the daily practice of wudu (ablution) may have inadvertent preventive benefits, practices like congregational gatherings, consuming cow urine, or insisting on physical contact like handshakes must be critically re-evaluated and abandoned. The coronavirus is a grave threat to our collective well-being, and the imperviousness of certain religious doctrines to scientific reasoning only deepens our vulnerability. To navigate this crisis effectively, religious traditions must evolve, prioritising human safety and rationality over archaic dogma.

Another possibility arising from the coronavirus pandemic is the emergence of a new hyper-real-world order. While this may initially seem speculative, the long-term psychological effects of the pandemic on human behaviour are undeniable. For this generation, the simple acts of touch, visiting crowded spaces, or even breathing in enclosed environments may no longer feel natural or safe. Physical distancing could become the new normal, prompting technologically advanced societies to increasingly rely on telecommunication, digital interfaces, and the manipulation of information.

In such a scenario, simulated realities—modern interpretations of Platonic ideal forms—may play a pivotal role in reshaping our understanding of the world. Virtual environments, augmented realities, and advanced digital tools may not only redefine human interaction but also influence how societies function, from workspaces to education, healthcare, and even social rituals. As hyper-reality gains prominence, it could challenge traditional perceptions of physical presence and authenticity, ushering in a reality where the boundary between the real and the virtual becomes increasingly blurred.

Furthermore, the coronavirus outbreak has cast a harsh light on the very phenomenology of love, empathy, and compassion. In a world dominated by sanctions, nationalism, and capitalism, these virtues—central to human connection— seem to have been relegated to irrelevance. The pandemic has exposed how systems prioritising profit, borders, and power often overshadow fundamental human values, leaving little room for collective care and solidarity during crises.

Yet, amidst this bleak reality, we must hold onto hope. Let us hope that the pandemic not only ends soon but also serves as a catalyst for profound change. It is an opportunity to rebuild a world where compassion, empathy, and love are no longer sidelined but actively shape our social, political, and economic frameworks. A better world is not just a possibility—it is an imperative.

14

RETHINKING PANDIT REHABILITATION

Diaspora, deracination, and displacement are age-old civilizational phenomena that have shaped human history and identity, often emerging from a variety of crises and motivations. These processes, though frequently viewed as contemporary challenges, are deeply rooted in the annals of time. Historically, they have been spurred by natural disasters, economic upheavals, political instability, wars, and even humanity's innate desire to explore and trade. In today's interconnected and politically charged world, however, displacement is increasingly driven by power dynamics, territorial disputes, and technological advancements, rather than by organic or moral predicaments. The deracination of the Kashmiri Pandit (KP) community in the early 1990s serves as a stark example of displacement induced by fragile political conditions rather than an inherent rupture in the age-old cultural and communal harmony between Kashmiri Muslims and Pandits. The exodus of KPs from their homeland was not just a tragic outcome of political instability but also a devastating loss to the region's rich composite culture. Amid the current political discourse surrounding their return, the proposal to create separate settlements for Pandits appears shortsighted and divisive. Instead of perpetuating segregation and further alienating an already displaced community, the government should prioritize rebuilding the social and cultural ties that once united Muslims and Pandits. A genuine revival of this communal kindredship, rather than isolation, holds the key to healing the wounds of the past and fostering a harmonious coexistence in the Kashmir Valley.

One can hardly deny that the collectivistic cultural ethos of Kashmir is incomplete without the presence of Kashmiri Pandits, whose historical, intellectual, and cultural contributions have been integral to the region's identity. Their return to their ancestral homeland is not only a matter of justice but a crucial step towards restoring the social and cultural harmony that defined Kashmir for centuries. The armed insurgency of the early 1990s forced the mass displacement of approximately 62,000 registered Kashmiri Pandit families, leaving an indelible scar on the collective memory of the Valley. Of these, 40,000 families endured decades of sub-human conditions in Jammu, 20,000 struggled in the tough and unforgiving climate of Delhi, while around 2,000 were scattered across the rest of India and abroad, striving to rebuild their lives in alien environments. Their prolonged suffering and the erosion of their cultural connection with Kashmir demand an unequivocal acknowledgement of their right to return. There is no logical or moral justification, nor any political manoeuvring, that can question the rightful reclamation of their homeland. Their reintegration into the Valley must be seen as a moral imperative and a collective responsibility to tend to the wounds of the past and pave the way for a more inclusive future.

It has been over two and a half decades since the mass exodus of Kashmiri Pandits, yet despite repeated promises and rehabilitation efforts by successive state and central governments, meaningful action on the ground remains elusive. The politicization of the issue has only widened the gulf between the two victim communities, further entrenching mistrust and division. Union Minister Jitendra Singh's assertion that "we have to create a conducive atmosphere where the Pandits feel prompted and inspired to go back to their place of birth" or claims about "infusing confidence" through transit camps where "Muslim migrants will also live with them" are emblematic of the political irony—or outright absurdity—that has plagued this issue. These declarations ring hollow, as both state and central governments are well aware that the divisive proposal of separate settlements for Pandits will do little to create an environment of safety, dignity, and mutual coexistence.

This redundancy in political rhetoric is not new. In April 2008, former Prime Minister Manmohan Singh announced a package of Rs. 1,618 crores aimed at offering jobs to Kashmiri Pandits, alongside additional assistance. Out of this, Rs. 218.46 crores were allocated for the immediate establishment of transit accommodations. Yet today, these camps resemble little more than "decorated slums," a grim testament to the failure of such initiatives to restore even a semblance of the once-glorious harmony between Muslims and Pandits in the Valley. Years since their inception, these accommodations stand as stark reminders of bureaucratic inefficiency and the inability to address the deeper social and cultural fractures caused by decades of conflict and displacement. True rehabilitation requires more than token gestures and hollow promises; it demands a genuine commitment to rebuilding trust and fostering an inclusive social fabric that transcends political expediency.

Separate Settlements and the Myth of a 'Conducive Atmosphere'

Amid the ongoing political confusion surrounding the return of Kashmiri Pandits, the two widely debated terms— "separate settlements" and "conducive atmosphere"— seem diametrically opposed. The pursuit of one ironically undermines the possibility of the other. Separate settlements, rather than fostering security or stability, are likely to exacerbate the already fragile living conditions in the Valley. Separate settlements risk creating isolated pockets that could become targets of resentment or violence, perpetuating a cycle of fear and division. Such policies contradict the principle of national integration. The failure of similar segregation policies in conflict zones worldwide, such as in Palestine or Bosnia, underscores the dangers of ghettoising communities. Such measures often exacerbate tensions rather than resolve them. Conversely, creating a genuinely conducive atmosphere for the return of Pandits is incompatible with the divisive and isolating nature of segregated colonies. In this political deadlock, it is the two communities—Pandits and Muslims— who continue to suffer, caught between unfulfilled promises and polarising rhetoric.

Instead of endorsing segregation, the government must focus on reviving the spirit of composite culture that once defined Kashmir's social fabric. The solution lies in encouraging both communities to reconnect with their shared, harmonious past rather than isolating one and labelling it as the "cultural other." In *The Garden of Solitude*, the first English novel by a Kashmiri Pandit, Siddhartha Gigoo poignantly captures the concord that once existed. He recounts how his grandmother and a neighbouring Muslim woman communicated "through the windows of the fourth floor of their houses while winnowing rice," an intimate reflection of the intertwined lives of Muslims and Pandits before the exodus.

The government's priority should be to rekindle such bonds of coexistence rather than fuelling division through the establishment of segregated settlements. The propaganda of separate settlements not only alienates the Pandit community further but also betrays the aspirations of the majority in both communities, who largely oppose such isolationist measures. Instead of uniting people, such plans risk deepening the already existing trust deficit, rendering reconciliation an even more distant dream.

Mehbooba Mufti's assertion that "once their (Kashmiri Pandits) confidence grows, they can live wherever they want" is emblematic of the lack of serious political understanding. Separate settlements, far from inspiring confidence, are likely to perpetuate fear and mistrust. History provides ample evidence: the 2008 transit camps, designed with similar intentions, did little to restore trust or foster a sense of security among Pandits. Instead, they left the displaced community psychologically trapped, ultimately leading the younger generation of Pandits to prefer life in Jammu over return to a fractured homeland. The younger generation of Pandits, born and raised outside Kashmir, faces a cultural disconnect. For them, the idea of "return" is more symbolic than practical, as they have little connection to the land their parents or grandparents once called home. Decades of separation and mutual suffering have eroded trust between the two communities, making reconciliation a complex and delicate process. Any attempt at rehabilitation must address this trust deficit as a priority.

Moreover, segregated settlements risk inflaming the already tense political climate. The separatist and insurgent groups, who vehemently oppose such measures as a form of "ghettoisation," may exploit the situation, escalating violence and further destabilising the region. As long as the conflict casts its shadow over daily life, the majority Muslim community itself remains precariously positioned, let alone the displaced and disoriented Pandit community.

What is needed is not segregation but integration—an effort to restore confidence through dialogue, cultural exchange, and a commitment to rebuilding trust. Only by addressing the root causes of mistrust and conflict can a truly conducive atmosphere emerge, one where Pandits and Muslims can live side by side as they once did, rather than as victims of divisive political agendas.

Rather than adhering to the divisive and opaque policies of the PDP-BJP coalition government, the Kashmiri Pandit community—particularly its younger, increasingly "de-cultured" generation—should focus on rebuilding bridges with the people of Kashmir through genuine dialogue. If they truly seek to revive the lost "composite culture" of the Valley, trusting and engaging with their Muslim counterparts is indispensable. The notion of rehabilitation through "inclusive" transit camps is nothing more than a politically expedient myth. Kashmir is the Pandits' homeland, and no external force should deter them from reclaiming their rightful place.

Farooq Abdullah's recent assertion that "no one in Kashmir [who] will go to Kashmiri Pandits with a begging bowl" underscores an important truth: the responsibility for returning to their roots lies with the Pandits themselves. However, their need for security should not stem from fear of the Kashmiri people, who have endured decades of suffering alongside them. Instead, their real threat lies in the political exploitation of the conflict by corrupt and opportunistic politicians.

The return of Pandits, while symbolically significant, cannot resolve the larger conflict. On the contrary, if handled poorly, it risks becoming a tool for political parties to deepen divisions and use Pandit enclaves as leverage to exacerbate an already fraught situation. True reconciliation and rehabilitation can only occur when the Pandit community refuses to be pawns in political games and instead embraces their shared history with Kashmir's Muslim population, working together to forge a more inclusive future.

The issue of the Kashmiri Pandits' return to their homeland transcends political manoeuvring and is fundamentally rooted in the people and their shared heritage. Sadly, the inverse is at play: politicians, driven by self-serving agendas, dominate the narrative, while genuine public sentiment is glaringly neglected. Both communities must recognize that decades of political exploitation have yielded little but a deepening crisis, with meaningful action conspicuously absent.

To conclude, Siddhartha Gigoo's poignant novel, *The Garden of Solitude*, offers a compelling reflection on the unity that once defined the Pandit-Muslim relationship, the harrowing conditions of Pandits in migrant camps, and their unrelenting yearning for home. As Gigoo writes, "We (Pandits and Muslims of Kashmir) have been betrayed by the government, by the uniformed men, and by the agencies which claim to be our well-wishers." This line aptly encapsulates the shared disillusionment of both communities and underscores the urgent need for them to reclaim agency over their future, free from the manipulations of divisive politics.

15

KASHMIR: A CASE OF DISCIPLINE AND PUNISH

In his seminal work, *Discipline and Punish*, Michel Foucault describes a system of control that operates through surveillance, categorisation, and the normalisation of power. He writes, "This enclosed, segmented space, observed at every point, in which the individuals are inserted in a fixed place, in which the slightest movements are supervised, in which all the events are recorded, in which an uninterrupted work of writing links the centre to the periphery, in which power is exercised without division, according to a continuous hierarchical figure, in which the individual is constantly located, examined and distributed among the living beings, the sick and the dead—all this constitutes a compact model of a disciplinary mechanism." This model of panopticism is a defining feature of modern states, where power is exercised through pervasive surveillance and institutional control.

To assess the relevance and truth of Foucault's assertion, the socio-political landscape of Kashmir provides a compelling case study. With its contested borders, fraught history, and ongoing political uncertainty, Kashmir fits well within Foucault's concept of an "enclosed, segmented space." The region has been subjected to continuous observation, categorisation, and regulation, creating a system of control that resonates with Foucault's disciplinary mechanism. Here, the hegemonic political control operates as a force that disciplines society through laws, policies, and institutional practices, ensuring compliance and subduing dissent. Over time, this mechanism has not only suppressed agency but also generated a complex discourse of power and knowledge—a Foucauldian apparatus that perpetuates itself through the very systems it creates.

The political nature of the state's ceaseless inspection and ubiquitous surveillance in Kashmir stands as a stark anomaly even within the broader framework of India's governance. What sets this mechanism apart—and makes it particularly insidious—is its reliance on historically coercive strategies aimed at institutionalising fear and psychological insecurity. This fear operates at multiple levels: the fear of the gun, of an encounter, of a massacre, of protests spiralling into bloodshed, of sudden explosions, of being a suspect, and ultimately, the existential dread of simply being Kashmiri. These fears, cultivated over decades, have seeped into the collective psyche, forming what can be termed as the psychic residue of Kashmir—a haunting legacy of the state's disciplinary mechanism.

The state's apocalyptic defence strategies and unchecked armed aggression have corroded the once-rich religious and cultural ethos of Kashmir, reducing it to a shadow of its pre-conflict vibrancy. The responsibility for this degeneration lies squarely with the state's domineering political culture, which has stunted the psychological growth of its people and reshaped their collective identity through a lens of violence and insecurity. Unlike other regions, the language, behaviour, and thought patterns of Kashmiris have been profoundly influenced by the state's oppressive apparatus, making it possible to distinguish a Kashmiri English newspaper from hundreds of others solely by its content and tone. This distinction lies not in linguistic style but in the pervasive undertone of fear, trauma, and resistance—a reflection of a society shaped by relentless surveillance.

The terms that dominate Kashmir's vernacular—firing, curfew, crackdown, ambush, grenade, encounter, strike, military, blast, camp—are deeply ingrained in the everyday lexicon, normalising violence for both children and adults. Nowhere else is this normalisation more apparent than in the play of Kashmiri children, who mimic soldiers with wooden guns slung over their shoulders, re-enacting military actions with cries of "thak, thak, thak." This chilling example underscores how the state's disciplinary mechanism not only regulates behaviour but infiltrates imagination, transforming even childhood innocence into a reflection of militarised reality.

Such manifestations reveal the overwhelming power of state-sponsored discourses, which shape consciousness in ways that leave the subject largely unaware of the process. By embedding fear and control into the social fabric, the state has effectively turned its disciplinary mechanism into a tool for producing docile, disoriented citizens—a generation conditioned to navigate life within the confines of state-imposed narratives and militarised existence. This dynamic underscores the urgency of questioning these mechanisms to reclaim the human and cultural ethos of Kashmir.

The fragmented and disoriented electorate of Kashmir stands as yet another grim testament to the success of the state's political machinery. This machinery has so thoroughly manipulated and nourished the political consciousness of the people that they often fail to grasp the fundamental question: why and for what purpose are elections held? The common sense of a Kashmiri voter is so mired in confusion that it readily succumbs to the hollow promises of politicians, who, as the satirical adage goes, vow to build bridges even where there are no rivers. Shakespeare's poignant lines from his sonnet aptly resonate with this predicament:

How with this rage shall beauty hold a plea,

Whose action is no stronger than a flower.

The state's political apparatus begins its work long before an individual is even born, embedding a preordained political identity and consciousness into the collective psyche. In Kashmir, this identity is not chosen but imposed, and it is burdened with suspicion and alienation. A Kashmiri is not born a suspect, yet in the broader Indian context, they are compelled to live as one. A powerful discourse perpetuates this notion, casting Kashmiris as inherently connected to militancy, Pakistan, and unconstitutional secessionism.

The former RAW chief A.S. Dulat's book, *Kashmir: The Vajpayee Years*, exemplifies how this overarching political machinery operates. While the book does not provide groundbreaking insights into Kashmir's political history, it does offer a candid glimpse into a "segmented space" stifled by relentless surveillance. A.G. Noorani, the eminent Indian lawyer and historian, aptly critiques Dulat's work:

"The book reveals all too clearly how in Jammu and Kashmir the intelligence agencies subverted the democratic process with intrigue and the electoral process with bribery and debased the quality of political life."

This critique underscores the systematic subversion of democracy in Kashmir, where the political and electoral processes have been reduced to tools of manipulation, bribery, and control. The state's disciplinary mechanism has not only contaminated the political landscape but also left an indelible mark on the individual psyche.

While disciplinary mechanisms are an indispensable part of governance globally, their manifestation in Kashmir is deeply flawed. In developed democracies, such mechanisms are internalized for the collective good, fostering trust and civic responsibility. In contrast, in Kashmir, they operate on a foundation of fear, coercion, and psychological manipulation. The deliberate misuse of power by the political-administrative apparatus exacerbates this crisis, perpetuating a cycle of distrust, alienation, and repression.

The solution to this systemic dysfunction does not lie in modifying or reconditioning individual consciousness alone. Rather, it demands a complete overhaul of the state's disciplinary mechanism, one that prioritizes the collective well-being of the people over control and domination. Without this fundamental restructuring, the internalization of such a mechanism will continue to produce a community riddled with confusion and intolerance.

If human good is the ultimate aim of any disciplinary system, then in Kashmir, this system urgently requires a radical transformation—one that fosters inclusion, trust and hope rather than fear and despair.

16

ON SUFFERING AND ATTACHMENTS

"We must suffer to the end, to the moment when we stop believing in suffering."

Emile M. Cioran

It is truly remarkable that we possess the ability to think, yet equally disheartening that we are susceptible to suffering. Happiness, in its true essence, does not exist in isolation. It necessitates its indispensable counterpart, for its significance would be impossible without its binary companion. We engage in thought, we take action, and consequently, we experience pain. Suffering arises from the incongruity between our thoughts and actions; there are instances when our actions fail to align with our thoughts, and conversely, our thoughts do not correspond with our actions. Prior to manifesting as actions, our thoughts journey through a vast realm of emotions and feelings. While thoughts and actions may transiently appear and fade away, the residue of pain they leave in their wake endures indefinitely. Moments of happiness, too, fleetingly pass us by, dissipating like cotton engulfed in flames.

Life, in its entirety, can often feel like an investment in suffering, with only fleeting moments of happiness as the return. In our pursuit of happiness, we exert all possible efforts, subjecting ourselves to immense hardship. Yet, when that transient moment of joy arrives, we tend to forget the pain endured and embark on a fresh journey, seeking further happiness. I witnessed this firsthand while closely observing my cousin's arduous journey in preparing for exams. He would neglect regular meals, fall asleep with a book in his hand, experience weight gain, constipation, and even haemorrhoids. Despite encountering numerous health issues, he persisted relentlessly for four consecutive months, subjecting himself to self-inflicted torture. Eventually, he achieved the top position in the results, and the happiness that followed lasted merely a few hours. The very next day, I found him already in search of something else.

Acknowledging that suffering is inevitable does not imply pessimism or an intransigent outlook on life. Similarly, acknowledging the potential for optimism or the belief that discovering inherent meaning in life can lead to true or everlasting happiness is not unfounded either. The coexistence of mutually antagonistic beliefs is a separate topic. Suffering is inherent and deeply woven into the fabric of our existence. From the moment of birth until our eventual passing, life shapes itself without granting complete freedom. Even if one were to achieve freedom, the secret or the knowledge to eternal happiness remains elusive. Slowly, living becomes entangled with various associations that significantly influence its course, imperceptibly sewing suffering into its very form. Suffering slowly wields immense power and control, subtly reducing the true purpose of life to mere acts of braving and overcoming it. It may sound absurd, but many of our plans and actions, to which we willingly and sometimes unconsciously submit, are actually small attempts to escape from pervasive suffering.

In order to understand suffering, it is necessary to understand its underlying causes. When we search for the causes, we will undoubtedly encounter the associations and attachments we form as living beings; even abstract associations have the potential to cause suffering. Our attachments, much like suffering, are inevitable and challenging to avoid. Although attachments are necessary in the places we are born, we tend to accumulate them without complaining about the suffering they may bring. However, does this imply that complete detachment can eradicate suffering? Not quite, as living without any attachment is nearly impossible. All attachments don't always bring suffering. However, it would be tough to contend that some attachments do not bring any suffering at all. Even if we detach, like the example of a recluse or a mountain hermit, it is often for a different form of attachment. Regardless of how blissful and healing ancient sanctified beliefs may sound, suffering cannot be entirely undone. It remains an undeniable reality, as clear as daylight. However, in acknowledging that suffering is an indispensable part of life, we can explore ways to minimize its impact on our individual selves. Can we achieve this? The answer should be yes. Let's delve deeper into understanding how.

Understating Suffering

Suffering can't be solely defined as someone undergoing pain or distress in a given moment. It pervades every moment, even when we don't feel we are suffering. The greatest suffering lies in the willingness to readily, without grumbling, accept and undergo hardship to attain a moment of happiness. First of all, with clarity of mind, we must acknowledge that suffering is not easily conquerable, echoing the words of the Austrian poet Rilke, who described it as "stubbornly imperishable." Rilke also believed that suffering persists, remains inaccessible yet clings on, envious of everything else and stuck in its own terrible reality. The understanding that suffering is nearly invincible or an inherent part of the human experience allows us to embrace its presence, much like we do with our attachments unconsciously, and enables us to develop resilience and a greater sense of compassion for ourselves and others. This awareness transforms suffering into something we can endure. When we acknowledge its inevitability, we can approach it with a more balanced perspective, accepting its presence without succumbing to despair.

Appreciation of Suffering

Arthur Schopenhauer, the renowned German philosopher, wrote against the absurdity of viewing the widespread pain in the world as purposeless or random, as it is inseparable from life's inherent needs and necessities. While individual misfortunes may seem exceptional, suffering itself is a common aspect of existence. Schopenhauer challenges the notion presented in many philosophical systems that evil is merely negative, asserting instead that it possesses a positive, tangible presence. It is essential to clarify that the intention here is not to advocate for or celebrate suffering, but rather to discourage the condemnation or rejection of suffering as inherently evil or divinely ordained retribution for sin. An alternative perspective on suffering invites us to appreciate it in a Keatsian manner. In his poem *Ode on Melancholy*, Keats beautifully employs the metaphor of rain falling to depict sadness enveloping an individual. Just as rain is essential for the survival and beauty of 'droop-headed flowers,' suffering can also serve a purpose in our lives. While it may seem to weigh upon us like rain on petals, it can lead to growth, resilience, and a deeper appreciation for the joys that follow. Thus, embracing suffering not as an inherently negative force, but as a part of life's transformative journey, can lead us to find meaning and strength in the face of adversity. While the notion of appreciating suffering in a Keatsian way might resonate with some, it may seem shallow to those who find themselves overwhelmed and unable to cope with persistent suffering. Even if individuals manage to emerge from a particularly difficult phase of anguish, it does not guarantee immunity from future hardships. Regrettably, suffering can persist, making it a formidable challenge to confront. Therefore, suffering calls for a positive approach and appreciation rather than denial or disdain as this can only exacerbate its impact. Allow me to quote Schopenhauer once more: "Long you must suffer, knowing not what, until suddenly out of spitefully chewed fruit your suffering's taste comes forth in you. Then you will love almost instantly what's tasted. No one will ever talk you out of it."

Understanding the Nature of Attachments

While it is not entirely impossible to prevent attachments from forming, it is also true that they can develop despite our efforts to avoid them. While some suffering may arise from natural causes like disease or natural calamities, a significant portion of our suffering emanates from these attachments. It is important to acknowledge that we cannot entirely escape the potential suffering that attachments may bring at any point in time. However, by gaining a deeper understanding of the true nature of these attachments, we can work towards minimizing their impact on our lives. Our attachments and their potential to cause emotional pain operate within a complex 'symbolic order' inherent in human society. This symbolic order is, in essence, an intricate network of signifying codes that seemingly influence the formation and nature of our attachments in a seemingly natural sequence. Understanding the profound influence of this 'symbolic order' can offer insights into the nature of human connections and how we navigate the potential pain that accompanies our attachments. By exploring these complexities, we can strive to foster healthier and more meaningful attachments while acknowledging the profound role of society in shaping our emotional landscapes. While we remain bound to enact our roles within this complex symbolic system and inevitably experience suffering, we can come to comprehend that the very framework governing our attachments is fundamentally constructed. This awareness has the power to shift our perceptions and enable us to evade deeper entanglements with such associations.

Conclusion

In conclusion, life's intertwined reality of thinking, action, and suffering poses a profound paradox. We must acknowledge the inevitability of suffering, yet understanding its underlying causes and appreciating its transformative potential can offer resilience and compassion. Moreover, by comprehending the artificial nature of attachments and their influence on our emotional landscape, we can strive to navigate life's complexities with greater awareness and minimize the impact of suffering on our individual journeys.

17

THE HIDDEN COST OF NEWS MEDIA DURING PANDEMIC

After listening to a psychiatrist outlining the psychological toll of extended home confinement amid the second wave of coronavirus in India, my thoughts veered towards the destructive influence of the news media, a force I had recently distanced myself from due to its ceaseless fixation on despair, tragedy, crime, and the grim spectacle of human suffering. While the psychiatrist refrained from indicting the institution of news media for the surge in psychotic and somatic complaints, I found myself unable to absolve it. In my view, its theatrical dramatisations and relentless negativity had become the primary trigger for a landslide of despair and hopelessness within me. The unyielding rampage of the virus had already created an existential void, severing my connections to the immediate, tangible world. This void was further magnified by the tormenting narratives propagated by the news media, which began to distort my perception of reality, infiltrating my thoughts and actions. The paradox of news media lies in its ability to allure and ensnare with the spectacular, regardless of its catastrophic implications. I had been morbidly drawn to its continuous cycle of despair until I realized it was suffocating my imagination, replacing possibilities with an unending deluge of agony. Let us delve into the undesirable aspects of this pervasive institution.

Obsession with the Macabre

Dismissiveness may be a general human tendency, but let my critique not be mistaken for an attempt to undermine the steadfast determination and relentless efforts of the news industry in disseminating critical information to an audience safely consuming it from their comfortable couches. That said, my mind, at some point, began resisting the insidious intrusion of morbid information, manipulated reportage, and haunting imagery broadcast by various news channels. For these outlets, it seems only the gruesome, disheartening, and overtly sentimental qualify as newsworthy. Anything imbued with promise, progress, or renewal rarely makes it past their editorial gates.

Their obsessive focus on burning crematoriums, patients writhing in agony, grieving attendants, and the relentless tally of the dead—be it from accidents, fires, encounters, cyclones, rapes, or murders—forms the backbone of their coverage. These macabre visuals are replayed incessantly, resonating in multiple languages across the country. It is not that death is foreign to human experience, but no one willingly bears witness to it unless compelled. And when collective despair and pervasive boredom lead you to encounter death so vividly on screen, it becomes impossible to sustain optimism or draw solace from utopian ideals of peace and happiness.

The unrestrained portrayal of death, accompanied by a cacophony of dramatic reportage, achieves no catharsis, no anagnorisis. Instead, it exacerbates confusion and dread in an already disoriented audience. In this, the news media strays far from its noble purpose of informing the public, resembling more a macabre spectacle designed to perpetuate fear and despondency.

Tone and Terminology

Indian academician Amit Abraham aptly noted, "The pen had been mightier than the sword, but then the tongue took over." In the realm of news media, where the tongue now dominates, the symbolic and connotative usage of words, signs, and expressions has become disturbingly unparalleled. It often seems that, as the saying goes, it is not what is said but how it is said. Many news channels play a rising, jarring tone in the background, which crescendos to an unnerving pitch as the news unfolds. What does this achieve? Perhaps it aims to earn higher ratings, convince viewers that news is no longer mere reportage but spectacle, or foster the notion that news thrives only amidst chaos, catastrophe, and calamity. Even if a viewer fails to grasp the deeper semantics, the tone alone suffices to instill a sense of urgency, despair, and disillusionment.

Beyond tone, the manipulation of terminology by the news media is equally disconcerting. With alarming swiftness, news outlets latch onto divisive phrases, sensational expressions, and polarizing terminology, dissecting them until their essence is entirely distorted. Like vultures circling carrion, they pounce on a politician's inflammatory remarks, a celebrity's ill-chosen words, or a corporate magnate's staggering earnings, chewing these morsels into unrecognizable interpretations. Consider how terms are framed: government becomes synonymous with unquestionable supremacy; dissent is debated as a threat to national unity; election morphs into a theatre of negative competition; coronavirus becomes the harbinger of inevitable death; and now black fungus is framed as an apocalyptic scourge.

In their stark dichotomies, as Aldous Huxley says, everything is painted "either diabolically black or celestially white." Such terminology does not merely inform; it shapes cultural associations and, by extension, collective consciousness. In a world already marked by precarious realities, the relentless repetition of divisive and despair-inducing terms can only deepen the cultural wounds. It suggests, implicitly or explicitly, that hope has been extinguished, leaving only a bleak landscape of despair. As Michel de Certeau also insightfully remarked, "The media transforms the great silence of things into its opposite." Instead of fostering understanding or resilience, it amplifies a cacophony of fear, robbing language of its potential to heal or unite.

Ideology and Prejudice

News media often positions itself in the middle ground, an ostensibly neutral space designed to shield it from criticism and confer legitimacy on its reportage. However, even the middle ground cannot escape the influences of ideology. Ironically, in the Indian context, news channels often mirror the ideological divides of the political elite rather than transcending them. In televised debates, the lines between moderator and debater blur, and what ensues is a cacophony of mutually antagonistic opinions. Rarely do such debates aim for resolution; instead, they fixate on policies and political leadership, as if the world beyond these issues ceases to exist.

Herbert Gans, in his seminal book *Deciding What's News* (1979), observes that "when all other things are equal, the news pays most attention to and upholds the actions of elite individuals and elite institutions." This insight aptly describes the Indian news media, where arguments are less about exploration and more about reaffirmation of ideological biases. The debates often devolve into attacks rather than constructive discourse. When logic falters, uncivilized declamations and verbal onslaughts fill the void, revealing the corrosive influence of prejudice and ideology.

Amartya Sen's quip that "prolixity is not alien to us in India" aptly describes the culture of endless debates in Indian newsrooms. Panellists, self-proclaimed experts, and party spokespersons engage in lengthy monologues to defend preconceived notions, often rooted in collective ideological echo chambers. The result is a deeply polarising spectacle that leaves a slow but lasting impression on the viewer's consciousness.

The danger lies not merely in the content consumed but in the insidious process by which the viewer absorbs underlying ideologies. News, therefore, ceases to be information; it becomes an apparatus of ideological transmission. This influence extends beyond television screens, shaping public discourse in everyday settings—on streets, in shops, and during casual conversations. The culture of divisive debates in media reproduces itself in society, exacerbating divisions and fostering conflict.

In the uncertain times we inhabit, it is imperative to limit exposure to this side of news media culture. Left unchecked, it risks infecting our consciousness with a strain far more pernicious than any virus. As French philosopher Louis Althusser rightly argued, ideology operates unconsciously, slowly moulding individual subjects. Once this unconscious interpellation shapes the mind, its influence is nearly irreversible. As the poet John Donne might have mused, you may "go and catch a falling star" or "get with child a mandrake root," but reshaping a consciousness warped by ideology remains an impossible feat.

18

Echoes from the Hills: A Gujjar Youth's Struggle for Identity in Modern Kashmir

I teach at a college perched on the crest of a hill in North Kashmir. From this vantage point, the view is nothing short of breathtaking. To the front, the shimmering expanse of Wullar Lake stretches out in serene beauty, while to the right and behind rise the dense, green mountains, majestic and unyielding. On the left lies the picturesque town, dotted with small clusters of homes, their tin roofs glinting under the sun. Beyond the town, hamlets cling to the mountainside at heights that are both awe-inspiring and intimidating. Every time I gaze up at those scattered homes, bathed in sunlight, I can't help but wonder about the lives of the people living there—how they endure, especially during the harsh Kashmiri winters.

One of my students, **Sahil Khatana (SK)**, comes from one such hamlet, nestled at what seems to be the most daunting of altitudes. He calls it Gujjar Pati. A few days ago, during the farewell event for the outgoing batch, he became the talk of the college. His mesmerising performance, a traditional dance to a Gojri song, captivated everyone. It was a dance that spoke of the rich culture and heritage of his community.

One day, as I sat on the college lawn, basking in the afternoon sun, I spotted him walking by and called him over for a chat. What started as a casual conversation soon turned into an impromptu interview. His confidence and the clarity of his responses were remarkable, and I was eager to learn more about his life.

I: So, where exactly do you come from?

SK: Gujjar Pati.

(Sahil raised his arm, pointing towards the towering mountain that stood like a sentinel behind our college. His eyes traced the path as if showing me the exact spot of his home nestled somewhere in the craggy heights.)

I: Is it difficult to reach your village? What about the connectivity?

SK: Yes, it is. The matador takes us part of the way, about two kilometres from my home, and drops us off. From there, I have to climb a steep, narrow gravel path every day. Maybe that's why I'm so slim, sturdy, and tall—it's a daily workout.

(Sahil smiled as he said this, his humour revealing the resilience behind his words.)

I: And what about the winters, when it snows or when someone in the family falls ill?

SK: Winters are tough, no doubt. But we've grown used to it. We don't often suffer from serious illnesses, but when we do, we manage. We carry the sick person to the point where the road ends and from there, it's easier to get them to medical help. It may look daunting from down here, but when you've lived it, it doesn't seem as difficult as it appears.

I: Sahil, you recently danced to a Gojri song during the farewell. It was distinct—both the song and the dance. They must be very popular in your village.

SK: They used to be, but not anymore. It's sad. Over the last few years, our traditional Gojri songs and dances have started losing their relevance. Hardly anyone appreciates them now. It's mostly the elderly who still prefer them. When I was around 8 or 10 years of age, the sound of a drumbeat could fill the whole Gujjar Pati with life. But now, even the drum is fading into silence.

I: A drumbeat that could fill the entire village with life? How was it so invigorating, and why has it become irrelevant now?

SK: (His eyes lit up as he remembered.) We have a distinct culture from the Kashmiri people. Our livelihoods, for the most part, depend on rearing cattle, especially sheep and goats. In the past, before winter set in and the heavy snowfalls blocked our movement, people would gather in groups to cut grass in the highlands, where it grew in abundance. And they didn't do it alone—drummers and singers would accompany them. The drumbeats gave them courage and energy, pushing them to work faster. The faster the beat, the quicker the grass was cut. The best drum bands were always in demand, and they earned good money. (He paused, smiling wistfully.)

SK: It wasn't just work—it was a celebration. People would joke and laugh about the 'competitions' in the fields all winter long. The drumbeats and Gojri songs were the soundtrack of our lives. But now, those sounds are fading. Until a few years ago, no wedding was complete without dancers moving to the rhythm of the drums and singing Gojri songs late into the night. The women would sing madrigals—special songs in pure Gojri—wishing happiness for the bride and bridegroom. But the madrigals are lost now too.

(Sahil's voice trailed off as if the weight of what was lost was too heavy to carry.)

I: What do you mean by your culture being different from Kashmiri? Aren't you Kashmiri?

SK: Well, that's what we call the people living in the plains who speak Kashmiri. Up where I live, we don't speak Kashmiri much, although we understand it. And when we do try to speak it in the plains, our accent—how we pronounce the words—often gets in the way, and sometimes we face discrimination or even humiliation because of it. Some of us are more comfortable with Punjabi or Pahari (a regional language spoken in the hills) than with Kashmiri. We speak Gojri, and sometimes we're referred to as 'Gojri' by those we call Kashmiri, but often in a dismissive or even mocking way. You see, Kashmiri people tend to think of themselves as superior, and we Gujjars (a traditionally nomadic ethnic group) are very aware of that. There's a clear disparity—a difference in status or treatment—between us. This divide is understood on both sides. Since we Gujjars know we're distinct, we often refer to the people from the plains as Kashmiri. Sometimes, we use it in a dismissive way too.

But there's more to it. Over time, this disparity has led to many of us, especially the younger generation, developing an inferiority complex (a persistent feeling of being less important or worthy than others). It's not something that happened all at once, but it's certainly happening. You can see it now in how we celebrate festivals, weddings, and cultural events. The younger girls prefer singing Kashmiri or Punjabi songs, thinking these are more modern, more refined, or advanced compared to our traditional Gojri songs. Sadly, the old traditions—like drum beating, dancing, and singing bands—are fading. Those performers, who were once the heart of our celebrations, aren't invited to weddings anymore. Now, DJs and Punjabi music dominate the events. Our cultural identity is changing, and it seems no one is worried about what's being lost.

I: That sounds like a profound change. Have you thought about how you could preserve your culture?

SK: Yes, it's something I think about often. Studying literature at the college opened my eyes to the power of language. I've always wanted to write about all of this. We don't have anyone representing us, telling our stories, especially in a powerful way. To truly represent a community, you need a language that can capture its essence and communicate it widely.

English, for most of us, is almost non-existent—people up in my village rarely know it, and they don't see its value. Kashmiri isn't spoken well by the Gujjars either, and writing in it is even more unlikely. So, there's a gap. Most of my people don't know how to preserve their culture in their own language. That's why I thought learning English, which is read and understood by the largest number of people globally, would be the best way to write about my people. Through

English, I want to capture what's happening to us—the slow erosion of our identity—and share it with the world.

I: Do you feel that your community is dispossessed or disowned?

SK: We don't even exist for most people—except when it's convenient. Take the elections, for example. Suddenly, a few things start appearing, like roads being fixed or promises being made. But here we are, in the 21st century, and I still have to climb two kilometres every day from where the matador drops me off. No one really complains anymore because no one listens. When you're deprived of basic facilities for so long, you don't just stay backward—you begin to accept that identity. It becomes internalized. And once that happens, it gets normalized. When that sense of backwardness becomes normal, you unconsciously start imitating those you perceive as more advanced. That's what we Gujjars do in relation to the Kashmiri. We might not openly admire them, but in subtle ways, we imitate their ways, and their customs.

I: If I'm not mistaken, the government has been trying to do more for the Gujjar community, like launching schemes and increasing job quotas. Isn't that helping?

SK: Yes, there are some benefits. But there's a big difference between providing temporary benefits and truly emancipating a community. Uplifting people means more than just offering schemes. It's about improving education, infrastructure, healthcare, and most importantly, preserving cultural identity. The problem is that most people don't even understand what it means to have a distinct cultural identity or how to preserve it. And it's painful to see that the system doesn't do anything to ensure that preservation. People aren't taught these values, and their ignorance isn't seen as a problem by the system.

(Sahil's voice grew more passionate, and his frustration was evident.)

SK: The people know hundreds of ways to protect their livestock from predators, but they don't know how to preserve their own identity. This ignorance isn't their fault—it's been socially constructed. When a system ignores you for so long, it doesn't just neglect your physical needs; it erases your sense of self. That's what we're going through.